WHERE DID WE GO WRONG?

WHERE DID WE
GO WRONG?

From the Gold Standard to Europe

ERIC ROLL

faber and faber

LONDON · BOSTON

First published in 1995
by Faber and Faber Limited
3 Queen Square London WC1N 3AU

Typeset by Datix International Ltd, Bungay, Suffolk
Printed in England by Clays Ltd, St Ives plc

© Eric Roll 1995

A CIP record for this book
is available from the British Library

ISBN 0–571–17460–4

2 4 6 8 10 9 7 5 3 1

To Freda

Contents

Preface

'If you could look into the seeds of time and say which grain will grow and which will not.'

William Shakespeare, *Macbeth*

This is an exercise in hindsight, which can be a harmless and agreeable indulgence. It does not, however, always provide an understanding of complex past events. There is no shortage of scholarly commentaries and analyses of the last seventy years of British history, enriched by biographies and memoirs of many of the prominent actors and by the steady disclosure of official documents under the thirty-year rule. Not everything is published; nevertheless enough has been – up to the beginning of the 1960s – to have provided researchers with a great deal of raw material on many past policy discussions and decisions, domestic and international.

It may be that eventually – allowing for the gaps which continued and often exaggerated secrecy under the guise of concern for security will leave – more of the detailed history of policy making in the last seventy years will become known. I doubt, however, whether the identification of errors of policy will be made easier or, even if it is, whether the deeper reasons for the commission of errors will become evident.

The material so far available does clarify some specific decisions, but it does not explain the broad sweep of the history of the period. It must be left to the more speculative philosophers of history to offer enlightenment.

To steer a sensible path between the thicket of detail – this or that decision on this or that matter of policy – and the bolder generalizations of social philosophers is not easy. I have nevertheless attempted to do so because I am not satisfied either that the meticulous review of every turn of policy can provide a coherent understanding or that the broad sweep of some seductive over-arching theory can by itself offer a convincing explanation. I have sought to find something less fragmentary than the former and more satisfactory to those who look for coherence than the latter.

This book is for the general reader. I have kept it as short as the subject permits. Most of the narrative and analysis in Part One has been limited to the essentials. In Part Two I have tried to examine further past policy errors to see whether their origins lie in certain common features of policy making.

I have omitted charts, tables and footnotes and have named only few politicians and officials who have played an active part in these developments, and economists who have commented on them.

It may help the reader to know of my own position as this history unfolds. I started as a student of economics, fortunate in doing so in an environment in which the theoretical aspects of economics and related social disciplines were heavily supplemented by considerable attention to applied economics and to both the history and the current trends of industrial, commercial and financial conditions. Later, I myself taught various aspects of economics, again with considerable attention to actual economic developments during the years of depression and after. I also had the opportunity to visit and work at a number of American universities and to travel widely in the United States and Canada.

During the war I was Executive Officer, later the British member of the Combined Food Board in Washington. For twenty years after the war I was concerned with many economic matters at home and abroad, including the change in economic policy from war-time and early post-war controls in food, agriculture and external financial policy to the gradual re-liberalization and reconstruction of the economy. This period included, in particular, many international negotiations, such as the Marshall

Plan, Nato and the Brussels negotiations. In all these the country had to adapt its policies, ambitions and aspirations to a vastly changed world environment. For the last twenty-six years, I have been active in the City in an investment bank and able to observe more directly the effect of economic developments and of changes in policy on the actual performance of the British economy, both in the financial sphere and in much of industry and trade.

I want to acknowledge generally my debt to a number of contemporary economists in universities, research institutes, central banks and government departments, with many of whom I have worked, as well as those of the regular commentators in the press, whom I respect. If they find – as they will – ideas similar to their own, I hope they will accept this anonymous acknowledgement of their influence.

LONDON   Eric Roll

PART ONE: How

'Great Britain should ... endeavour to accommodate her future views and designs to the real mediocrity of her circumstances.'

Adam Smith, *The Wealth of Nations*

'They (politicians) know how much of the art of politics lies in concealing behind a façade of rigid adherence to immutable principles those deviations or reversals, events and responsibility so often force on governments.'

Robert Blake, *Disraeli*

As the century approaches its end, it seems worthwhile to review its course so far. I have, however, limited myself to roughly the last seventy years, 1925 to 1993. The year 1993 is a convenient terminal as it is the year in which the single European market came into being, thirty-five years after the European Community was started and twenty years after Britain joined it. As I start to write this account, the single market is far from perfect, and Britain is still in the grip of an economic recession that at one time threatened to become one of the gravest this century. As I finish it, signs of improvement have begun to appear, but even the most optimistic forecasters expect unemployment to remain a grave problem for some years.

Instead of the glorious new phase of European integration that was to follow formal arrival of the single market, there is now great uncertainty over the future of the European Community, or Union as it is now called, not least because of continuing confusion about what the attitude of Britain towards it really is. And as for us, neither Schadenfreude over the suddenly revealed weakness of economic giants like Germany and Japan, nor our finger-pointing at others also in the grip of uncertainty over Europe, such as even Germany and France, helps us with our economic troubles or political uncertainties. As what follows will show, our record during two-thirds of a century should oblige us to undertake a meticulous objective self-examination.

As for my starting date, 1925, it happens to be the year in which I came to Britain at the age of seventeen and at once became interested in the country's economic past, present and future. More important, however, it is also the year in which the phase of reconstruction after the First World War ended; and the short-lived first Labour government too; the gold standard was restored; and the great Empire Exhibition at Wembley was on – symbols of a return to 'normalcy'. Everything British seemed to me to be the acme of economic achievement and civilized progress. It was only later that I appreciated that as far as the economy was concerned, the seeds of decline were already at work.

The Performance of the Economy

The economy is nowadays overwhelmingly the main subject of general concern and public debate. Its current condition and future prospects preoccupy anyone who has the country's well-being at heart.

The history of people's preoccupation with these questions goes back virtually to the beginnings of economics as a systematic study itself, but it does not reach flood proportions until the period here reviewed. Although complaints about economic decline are frequently found in nineteenth-century literature, they have become much more common this century, particularly so in the last few decades. In recent years, a supposition (explicit or implicit) that there is something wrong with the British economy underlies most of what has been written about it. At the very least, its performance is usually considered to have been highly uneven, the fashionable phrase to describe this being 'stop-go'. Occasionally, it is the absolute performance that is regarded as inadequate, but the vast bulk of recent literature of dissatisfaction tends to be more concerned with Britain's relative performance, that is, how it compares with that of other countries of a similar level of economic development.

There is clearly much evidence – indeed more than prima facie evidence – to justify dissatisfaction. This is so, even if one accepts that Britain, the first highly industrialized country, the workshop of the world, could not have maintained its pre-eminent position for nearly two centuries in the face of all the technological, demographic, political and broad cultural changes of that

4

period. Most of the relevant statistics undoubtedly show a relative decline. This applies to such indices as gross domestic product (GDP), international trade, export performance and productivity from the beginning of the century to the late 1980s – and particularly in the last thirty years.

At this point two examples must suffice. In 1900 Britain ranked third in total GDP and third in GDP per caput. She also ranked first in exports. In 1987 she was eighth in GDP (fifteenth on a per caput basis) and fourth in exports. The most recent Organization for Economic Co-operation and Development (OECD) study confirms these data. In 1990 Britain ranked eighteenth out of twenty-four developed countries by income per head ($15,720 compared with $21,440 for the richest, the United States) and behind Italy, Australia, Norway, Iceland and the Netherlands.

The International Balance and the Return
to the Gold Standard

My starting point is the return in 1925 to the gold standard at the pre-war parity, a move which owed something to American pressure. By that year, the immediate effects of the First World War had been largely overcome. The economic consequences of the enormous losses in human life, particularly the virtual disappearance of the generation which would have furnished the leaders in the next phase of the country's development, are difficult to quantify. They certainly continued to have a depressing effect on economic and social enterprise and innovation for some years. This was probably more significant in Britain than in Germany and France. A somewhat less traumatic experience in this respect in the United States no doubt contributed to her spectacular economic development, leading ultimately to an unchallengeable international pre-eminence.

The actual transition to a progressive peace-time economy was far from smooth. Social discontent, very marked in the immediate post-war years, had abated by 1925, but a powerful residue was there in the form of a more radical trade union movement, which the short-lived experiment of a Labour government did little to satisfy. The reduction of overseas food supplies during the war was soon forgotten, and not remembered until the much more traumatic experiences fifteen years later, when it had a profound influence on agricultural policy.

Without a doubt, this one decision to return to the gold standard affected – and for the worse – the whole course of the economy, including export industries, notably coal. Its social and political consequences continued right through the 1930s, even beyond the relative recovery that set in, say, from 1933 onwards. It involved an increase of about 10 per cent in the external value of sterling and meant to all intents and purposes 'a policy of reducing everyone's wages by 2s in the £', as Keynes pointed out in his celebrated 1925 article, 'The Economic Consequences of Mr. Churchill'. No one can say for certain how these economic disturbances would have worked out had the surrounding political landscape – the rise of Fascism and Nazism, the Stalinist epoch, the Spanish Civil War, the American New Deal and the profound change in the world's economic and political power parallelogram – been different during those fifteen years. What is reasonably certain is that the evident economic troubles of Britain (at that time economically still a world power) made an important contribution to destabilizing the world economy. They greatly reduced Britain's inner strength and her ability to intervene effectively in a beneficent way during a period when world depression and political degeneration reigned, which culminated in the Second World War.

One domestic consequence particularly deserves to be recalled: the polarization in industrial relations which continued, with ups and downs, from the mining lockout and the General Strike, itself directly attributed by many to the loss of exports markets for coal, that resulted from the appreciation of sterling. While halted during the war, it afterwards led inexorably to increased expectations, and not only in regard to living standards. In the macro-economic sphere it resulted in periodic sharp clashes between the pressure for wage increases and the attempt to maintain price stability. Inflationary pressures caused by wage demands were a recurrent danger, and various attempts were made to deal with it, either under the broad heading of incomes policy or under the general policy towards trade unions.

These expectations also showed up in terms of industrial organization and public policy, imposing a heavy burden both on the economy and on the social and political fabric of the country. It included the status of trade unions in economic policy making, which markedly increased in the Labour governments of the 1960s and 70s. There was a perhaps inevitable sharp over-reaction in the 1980s, and some faint traces of yet another turn at the beginning of the 1990s.

Perhaps its only positive result is that it stimulated intense discussion of monetary problems, not only in the academic community, but also in the political world and in a wider public. In particular, the effect of exchange rate policy on foreign trade and domestic economic activity, partly through its direct effect on the trade and payments balance and partly through its consequences for monetary and fiscal policy, was from that time on never far from the centre of public debate. It was increasingly recognized that the effects of a major change in the exchange rate continued for a considerable time, and set in motion changes of actions and attitudes throughout the economy which could not easily be stopped. It is interesting to observe that a distinguished Japanese economist, Professor Tsuru, has argued that the setting of the yen/dollar exchange rate in 1949 (not altered until 1971) helped, after a time-lag, to 'stimulate Japan's manufacturing exports', and thus turned out to be perhaps the most seminal decision in shaping the post-war course of the Japanese economy.

It is worth recalling that the late 1920s and early 30s were also marked by a very uncertain handling of the great foreign policy issues, including economic ones, such as reparations (so very different after the Second World War), and the appeasement

7

of Mussolini and Hitler. This mishandling was the counterpart to the clinging to old doctrines of economic policy, of which '1925' was the first outstanding example.

We could have entered the war in an even weaker position than we did but for the belated recognition of the Fascist menace, the rearmament programmes and the improvement in Britain's terms of trade through the collapse of raw material and food prices (with, of course, their harmful secondary effects on primary producing countries and, thus, on our overseas markets).

The Great Depression and the Turbulent 1930s

In addition to the effects of the fatal error of 1925, there were other forces at work that produced the Great Depression in Britain early in 1931. Many of these originated in America, from where the great Wall Street crash of 1929 sent shock waves all over the world. It was responsible for the collapse of the largely American-financed, and often irrational, German reconstruction projects, and other financial phenomena, such as the failure of the Austrian Creditanstalt. To these were added a sharp decline of raw material and food prices that hit the agriculture of developed countries and, even more disastrously, less developed countries all over the world. The resultant restrictionist developments in world financial markets and growing protectionism in trade had the aggravating and self-defeating consequences which were then not as widely recognized as being the evils they are considered to be in modern thinking.

In Britain these developments overtook an economy already enfeebled by the existence of a grossly over-valued currency and its baleful balance of payments consequences, which steadily diminished London's liquidity and, therefore, its stability as an international financial centre. Above all, the lack of competitiveness induced by the 1925 decision resulted in a steadily rising volume of unemployment, which by the end of 1930 had reached the unprecedented total of $2\frac{1}{2}$ million.

The consequences of economic stagnation were those with which we were to become so painfully familiar at various points over the next six decades. Falling tax receipts combined with increased expenditures, particularly for unemployment benefits, created a large budget deficit (it was at that time not yet called the 'public sector borrowing requirement') which gave rise to major political disputes within the Labour government, and between it and both the Conservative and Liberal oppositions. The domestic crisis was soon supplemented – if not overshadowed – by an international one: the loss of confidence of the inter-national financial community, particularly the transatlantic one, threatened the stability of sterling and pointed to the clear danger that Britain would be unable to raise temporary financial support abroad.

The ensuing debate about how to deal with our woes was not startlingly different from what we experienced in later crises. Even the vocabulary of it is sometimes curiously similar. Thus, in 1931, the cry of 'a banker's ramp' was echoed between 1964 and 1966 by references to the evil machinations of the 'gnomes of Zurich', and the injunction in the late 1960s and 70s to cut unnecessary expenditure and to increase taxation could have been couched in the terms used more than thirty years earlier by Philip Snowden, Labour Chancellor in the government that had to face the crisis, and yet still have been easily understood. Incidentally, Snowden continued in this post in the first 'national' government that emerged as a result of it.

A much-used device was employed in the process of giving the government the basis on which to construct an emergency budget that would restore 'sound' finances and foreign confidence in the British financial system, and so prevent a departure from the gold standard. This was the setting up of a committee under Sir George May, a well-known City figure, whose report was pro-duced with remarkable speed, and whose recommendation for draconian measures popularized a new version of an old song: 'Here we come gathering noughts with May.'

The objective of preserving the gold standard, i.e. the convertibility of sterling at the existing parity, is probably the most revealing indicator of how deep-seated certain pre-conceived ideas were. (We shall encounter them again a number of times as we proceed towards 1993.) In a broadcast on 11 September, quoting remarks of the Liberal leader, Walter Runciman (who achieved additional notoriety as a negotiator with Hitler over Czechoslovakia), Snowden referred to the inflationary consequences of going off the gold standard and added that 'this is a menace to which British money has been alarmingly exposed in recent weeks. Action has been taken by the government in co-operation with the Bank of England which has averted such a terrible catastrophe.' Nine days later, on 20 September 1931, the government decided 'temporarily' to suspend the gold standard, with the effect that we had a floating exchange system up to the outbreak of war.

The 1931 resolution of the economic crisis, which brought about a radical change in the political landscape, somewhat transformed the character of but did not close the economic debate that had preceded it, one important focus of which was on the means of curing unemployment. Perhaps its most important point of focus was on the proper direction of fiscal policy at different points in the economic cycle, with which went a debate on the related international exchange rate régime, not only for Britain herself, but, given the American abandonment of the gold standard and the Roosevelt New Deal, for the world. Not surprisingly, Maynard Keynes condemned the May Committee's report as 'the most foolish document I have ever had the misfortune to read', and the budget based on it as 'replete with folly and injustice'. He was sure that the progressive consequences for the volume of employment and the receipts of taxation were bound to be bad. The suspension of the gold standard, to whose existence Keynes had reconciled himself, was the only result of the whole process that gave him any satisfaction.

It is worth looking further at the intellectual basis behind the powerful reactions of so many leading politicians and so much of the press, the City and the world financial establishment, and on which Keynes's vehement opposition was focused. Although the government did not actually present its case with a powerful dose of quotations from Adam Smith, its position can most simply, if crudely, be related to a famous Smithian dictum, namely, that the principles of the prudent conduct by the master of a family 'can scarcely be folly in that of a great kingdom'.

It is precisely the question of whether or not this is always, or even usually the case that underlies modern economic thinking, and is particularly linked with the Keynesian contribution. It is not necessary here to explain in detail how the process of the creation of the national income, its size and that of its constituents is explained, nor the effect on it of different directions of government policy, or how fiscal policy in particular can influence it, and how and why all this differs from the 'prudent conduct' of an individual household. Suffice it to say that more expansionist or more restrictive fiscal policies do not always have the same results. These depend on the state of the national income and its constituents, and in the main vary according to whether resources are fully employed or under-employed. It follows, therefore, as it did for Keynes and many others, that the expenditure cutting and revenue increasing measures of the 1931 government were exactly the contrary of what was needed when the unemployment level was over 2 million and the world generally was suffering from a severe depression.

Many observers would now class what happened in 1931 as a major error in economic policy which not only retarded economic recovery and enfeebled the economy at a time when the threat of war grew daily greater, but also added to the social tensions generated in the late 1920s. The net effect was to weaken that social cohesion which is particularly necessary when difficult economic choices, let alone political ones, have to be made.

The floating of sterling can be put on the favourable side of the account, as it facilitated a degree of internationalization of the monetary regime in 1936, when a tripartite monetary agreement took place between the American, British and French governments, to which some other governments rallied. Although not free from difficulties in execution, there was now at least a greater degree of international monetary co-operation which lasted virtually to the outbreak of war.

One other point belonging to the period of the 1930s may be mentioned, one which concerns the organization and structure of the domestic monetary system. Like so much of our economic history, it can be briefly summarized by a description of the setting up and the report of a Committee of Enquiry, on this occasion the Macmillan Committee on Finance and Industry, set up under a judge in 1929. It was composed of distinguished public figures, civil servants, politicians, trade unionists and economists, including Keynes, and it reported in June 1931, which makes it relevant to the other events that were set in train by the crisis of that year. The Treasury and the Bank appear to have tried to prevent the setting up of this committee, fearing that it would lead to the further spreading of discontent and questioning of the monetary system, and particularly its relation to the sorry state of industry through so much of the late 1920s and the gathering storm clouds of the forthcoming slump. The minority Labour government, however, felt that such an enquiry would at least demonstrate recognition of and concern about the economic situation.

In fact, although the main thrust of the Committee's enquiry may initially have been the constitution, organization and functioning of the Bank of England, the development of the slump and the approach of the 1931 crisis clearly influenced the report. Its recommendations, in so far as they related to new institutions with greater devotion to providing credit for industry and others (either actually made or hinted at) which related more to the Bank itself, were overshadowed by the crisis. There was much in this report that would have been useful in the reform process, but it was lost for quite some time, and contributed to the slowness of adaptation and the redressing of earlier policy. The new, expansionist ideas of Keynes were, however, already discernible in the report and even more in the minutes of the Committee's discussions, which show that they were by no means unchallenged. Perhaps one of the most significant of the opposing attitudes expressed by Lord Bradbury, the only dissenting member of the Committee, who had been a Permanent Secretary of the Treasury, is worth quoting from a number, all of which have contemporary echoes: among 'the main causes of the economic troubles of Great Britain', he cited, was 'the attempt by all classes to maintain a standard of living higher than is justified by the facts of the economic situation'.

The Second World War, the New Power Pattern and the European Recovery Programme, 1939–52

The recovery from the low point of the depression was inevitably slow. On the financial front, the immediate pressures were relieved not so much by the spate of economic conferences, even though less orthodox ideas started to assert themselves, but by greater co-operation between a number of European countries, as a result of their common experiences. The foundation of this co-operation was the willingness of the United States to help prevent a general collapse, something which could only be achieved with her help. The struggle to realize this greater spirit of co-operation and to understand the means by which co-operation could be made operative were constantly hampered by an opposite tendency towards protectionism and 'beggar-my-neighbour' policies. In the end this led to the collapse of the World Economic Conference, to the increased protectionism of the United States and the equally shortsighted Commonwealth trade policies.

For Britain one important factor which helped to counter the effects of the depression was a major turn in the terms of trade. The decline in raw materials and food prices had, at least in the short run, a favourable effect on Britain's trade terms. In the longer term, the consequent further impoverishment of the primary producing countries was, of course, disastrous not only for them but, through the ensuing financial crises and loss of export markets, for the industrialized, developed countries as well. Many devices were tried to sustain food and raw material prices, such as production quotas or price limiting schemes, but their net effect up to the outbreak of war was not really significant.

The world thus approached the war in an economically enfeebled state, with virtually only the United States, in any better condition. It had reacted to the ravages of its own depression (with hunger marches on Washington as significant a phenomenon as those from Jarrow to London) with a more comprehensive and innovative economic policy than any other country. Whether the Roosevelt New Deal was in all respects economically impeccable, or whether its work creating programmes and concurrent financial reforms would by themselves have produced lasting prosperity cannot now be said. However, what it certainly did was to create a far more effective basis for mobilizing the nation's resources, first to help the allies' war effort, then to participate actively in the war and, finally, to dominate it, with enormous consequences for the world's future power pattern.

To examine Britain's own war effort in terms of policies that have subsequently been revealed as wrong and responsible for inadequate performance is not relevant. 'Now thrive the armourers' stills most other considerations. It has been argued here and there that financial mobilization of resources abroad and their management here might have been speedier and more skilful; or that some rationing devices could have been introduced sooner. I do not think that any of these criticisms are proven or significant. Indeed, in many respects, the war-time management had clearly benefited greatly from the lessons of the First World War. It was remarkably effective in getting the most out of available material and human resources and directing them towards the war effort; and it achieved this together with the creation and maintenance of a spirit of social cohesion and a perception of fairness which could hardly have been bettered.

Of course, the total mobilization of resources that had become necessary (and accepted) this time, including direction of labour, was of a very different order from anything that took place under previous policies, and showed that a government faced with the horrendous dangers of total war, in this case against fascism, could quickly accept and implement even the most drastic changes after only short hesitation. In the financial sphere some controversy surrounded the speedy adoption of exchange control and the mobilization of overseas financial resources. However, even these hesitations were soon swept aside, and any hankering after preservation of 'normalcy' disappeared. That the American element was essential in the end, particularly from 1943 onwards, does not alter the basic picture, but it does show how massive an impact on the economic, to say nothing of the political, substance of the nation it made, and how profoundly it changed our relation with the United States.

The immediate post-war period, 1945–52, coincided with that of the first British Labour government to have a solid majority in the House of Commons, and also the first to be based on a strong wave of popular support for its general reforming approach to social questions, if not for all the specific items in its programme, and to a much less degree for the economic and financial measures which went with it. The broader questions of the general direction of this programme and its effect on the recovery will be better treated at a later stage as part of the general issue of how far alternations, real or apparent, in the social philosophy of political parties and their programmes have affected economic performance.

Here it is to be noted that in retrospect the harvest of those years seems a curious mixture of some major structural and operational changes, some of them new, others a simple continuation of practices imposed by war-time needs, together with as rapid as possible a return to 'normal', i.e. pre-war methods. The great accretion of new recruits to the Civil Service was fairly rapidly reversed; and, with the disappearance of rationing and other effects of the 'bonfire of controls', large segments of departments were quickly dismantled. The 'sponsoring' functions of ministries *vis-à-vis* certain sectors of industry, trade and finance also lost their justification, as allocations, priorities and the granting of import and export licences were eased or totally abolished and exchange control restrictions slowly but ineluctably eased.

If a fairly logical pattern (a kind of retrospective rationalization) is imposed on these developments, they appear as an attempt to dismantle as far and as quickly as possible the micro-economic elements of government policy while strengthening the macro-economic ones, as in the nationalization of the Bank of England and the extreme cheap money policy, and elements in fiscal policy with an expansionist orientation.

That all this was not successful either in creating a 'new Jerusalem', as some of the younger bright spirits in the government hoped, or in restoring what was still vigorous in the pre-war pattern of economic activity, is demonstrated by the fact that the ruling party lost the support of the electorate by the end of 1951 and was succeeded by the other major party for the unprecedented period of twelve years.

The Post-War Settlement

What is remarkable is that, in the midst of the pressures and hazards of war, some of the best minds were already turning to the problem of identifying and analyzing the post-war domestic and international situation and prescribing ways of dealing with it. There is strong evidence that, before 1945, policy makers, opinion formers and the general public alike had shaken off most of the backward-looking attitudes common in the decade after the First World War and the mixture of uncertainty and torpor of the late 1930s. This is not to say that all the ideas, political, social and above all economic, of that new dawn were universally accepted, let alone put into practice, but at least it showed that there was a readiness to think of new ways and to look at the post-war situation with a fresh mind.

Unfortunately, in certain crucial respects this new vigour was soon dissipated, or combined with old attitudes with even more unfortunate results than before. Basically, there was a failure to recognize, let alone take the measure of, the profound changes made and continuing to be made in the creation of the new world economic and political power maps. Domestically, while ideological differences were sharpened, the pattern of political methods remained virtually unchanged. The upswing that followed the 1945 election was soon dissipated. At the same time a determined drive took place to combine the shrinkage of the administrative apparatus, which the disappearance of many war-time controls, particularly rationing made possible with a reversion to pre-war civil service methods. Happily this was not wholly successful (or, to be fair, not pursued *à outrance*); and some measure of the freshness of approach and of the intellectual methods imported into the service during the war, together with some of the individuals responsible for them, were preserved.

Internationally, attitudes and policy were confused. They mirrored the uncertain state of the new, but not as yet clear-cut, patterns of economic, political and military power. This uncertainty, although also present elsewhere, seemed to affect particularly Britain's conduct of her post-war diplomacy. New questions were clamouring for resolution: What should the attitude be to the Commonwealth, old and new? How to react to the pressure for European integration, a movement with long antecedents, but powerfully renascent after the war? How to deal with the overwhelming power of the United States, now clear beyond any doubt, not only in the strategic sphere, especially after the descent of the Iron Curtain, but perhaps even more significant, and difficult to relate to, in economic and financial matters?

These difficulties became very clear in the course of the international negotiations over the Marshall Plan and after. The five-year period from the Marshall speech in 1947, and the coming together of the European countries to formulate a recovery programme with American assistance, to the official end of the programme in 1952, and the putting in place of a permanent inter-governmental organization (which also saw the end of the

17

first post-war Labour government and the beginning of twelve years of Conservative rule), was a particularly unsettling one.

The interrelation between domestic and international policy objectives was very marked. Two may be mentioned as outstanding examples: one, the obligations assumed under the Lend-Lease and Loan Agreements with the Americans, particularly the return to sterling convertibility, and two, the settlement with the holders of sterling balances, largely arising from the war. This time sterling convertibility (soon abandoned) was more obviously due to American pressure than the policy error of 1925. The problem of the sterling balances required tough and complex technical negotiations, which were complicated by psychological factors. Our attitude was a mixture of an anachronistic *grand-seigneurial* pose, a hankering after an unsustainable powerful international position for sterling, and indignation over the claims of creditors, who had mostly escaped the rigours of war, against a debtor who had heroically borne great war-time sacrifices. To grapple with all this would have taxed the intelligence and steadfastness of even the most solidly placed and most gifted government.

The resolution of these difficult issues was complicated by the demands of domestic programmes that were under even more pressure to create a land 'fit for heroes to live in' than were those after the First World War. This applied not only to social improvements, but was also reflected in the programmes for nationalization and enhanced worker participation in policy formulation. It showed up even more in the actual competitive demands for real resources for economic purposes, both domestic and for exports, and for international ones, notably the maintenance of strategic and foreign policy positions, and more specifically defence under the Nato programmes. These choices were extremely difficult to make; but whatever the detailed pattern might have been, the essential fact is that the sum total of the resulting claims on resources was clearly beyond the capacity of the economy. Prestige – even though the real value of it can at times be quite considerable – played too important a part when a balance of claims had to be struck; and this was true of decisions made by Labour and Conservative governments alike.

The role we played during the war and the achievement of victory were still most potent factors in the minds of policy makers and general public alike, and caused us to take a superior attitude both to former enemies and to those allies who had been occupied. As far as the United States was concerned, while no thinking person would have questioned the indispensable part played by it in the victory, this fact itself, and the subsequent overwhelmingly strong position of the United States, was not easily absorbed into thought and policy. The primacy of the United States had inevitably to be accepted, but in some quarters it was accompanied by an unhappy mixture of jealousy and resentment. At the same time this was combined with an insistence on our special relationship, of which more later.

It would be easy, but misleading, simply to ascribe the tergiversations of our conduct to our much reduced status and to the inevitable difficulties which were the consequences of a loss of power. Even in the era in which 'super-powers' began to emerge, when the real ties of Commonwealth were eroded and when there was ever-growing pressure for a coalescence of economic and political power on the European continent, the power of Britain, moral, intellectual, economic and financial, as well as political and military, remained for a remarkably long time very great indeed. It was moreover virtually unaffected by changes of government. However, even during the decade from 1952 onwards (a relatively more stable period), the different sources of our power were increasingly losing their efficacy, and so too were the methods open to us to apply what individual forms of power we actually still commanded. While few people during that period would actually have expected Britain to be able to influence world events by sending a cruiser to the River Plate or a gunboat up the Yangtse, our practical approach to many problems was until the end of that decade still much influenced by mental attitudes derived from earlier times when power relationships were different and our own power far greater.

This is perhaps most clearly seen in the first two post-war years when, on the one hand, the completion of the American loan negotiations promised relief from the painfully pressing balance of payments problem, while, on the other, clamour for resources for domestic against international purposes was becoming more and more strident.

In February 1946, when the American loan was not yet secured, though in his words 'quite safe', Keynes, in setting out in detail prospective international demands – relief in Europe, funds to deal with refugees and emigration, demands of the British Zone in Germany, grants and loans to colonies and other countries, military expenditures overseas, plus any net cost of releasing sterling balances – wrote that the figures 'are extremely shocking. . . . Ministers should not remain unwarned that they are going down the drain at a great pace.' It was at this point that American aid in the form of the Marshall Plan came to the rescue. It is irrelevant to enquire into the motives that impelled the United States to furnish – not on ordinary commercial loan terms – the wherewithal in the shape of many, many billions of dollars which restored badly degraded standards of living and supplied the essential materials and equipment for reconstructing a shattered productive machine. Concern for the re-building of the world's economic machine was certainly present, as was the desire to recreate in the longer run markets for American industrial and agricultural products, but a genuine and powerful ingredient of generosity towards allies who had suffered particularly from the war was also there; and this was strongly reinforced by the fear of what the political future of these same allies would be if they were not able to restore their economies.

As so often happens, the generous donor did not get the thanks his actions deserved. In part, there was in Europe resentment and fear of American might. And in part, the conditions attached (though rarely in a particularly stringent way) to the donation in regard to general policies – freer trade and financial conditions, a brake on more extravagant experiments in domestic policy with a general emphasis on traditional elements of prudence – aroused opposition. The conditions either ran counter to then common political attitudes and aspirations – as in the British Labour government – or they were simply regarded as designed to create an environment propitious for American trade and financial competition.

However, these were not the most important or the most lasting consequences of the plan. On the plus side it restored the foundation of the economy by easing the balance of payments constraints and created a new series of issues of common concern across the Atlantic, particularly after the creation of Nato and the inclusion of the defence dimension in an American/European mechanism.

From a British point of view, the period was nevertheless fraught with considerable economic problems, not all of which can be said to have been handled with the necessary skill. The perennial question of the exchange rate and the balance of payments continued to be uppermost, and the proceeds of the American loan, followed by the first big tranche of Marshall aid, did not stave off the difficulties. Many things continued to weigh heavily on the balance of payments and the exchange rate, like the extended liberalization of trade under the European Recovery Programme; the excessively generous settlement of the sterling balances; the confused and long unresolved concept of the sterling area in both its financial and trade aspects; and the heavy demands of the defence programme, particularly that of 1949, on the very industries on which success of the export drive depended. The devaluation of 1949, prepared a remarkably long time before it happened, provided only temporary relief, and by the end of 1951, Clement Attlee, to the surprise of his principal colleagues, who were at the time attending a Nato Council in Ottawa, called an election in which Labour was ousted.

The effect which the first taste of government, with its clash between preconceived aims and harsh economic realities, had on the future attitudes inside the Labour movement was possibly one of the more important long-term developments of this post-war period. The twelve years in opposition that followed only

21

deepened the movement's sense of frustration and uncertainty. This state of affairs had a marked influence on the internal struggles within the Labour Party and its ability to deal with the continuing economic problems when it once again became a party of government in the 1960s.

Reconstruction, Normalcy and the Mirage
of the Golden Age, 1952–70

I am grouping together in the following pages an exceptionally long segment of the post-war period. This requires some qualification. The first twelve years were dominated by Conservative governments which, notwithstanding some economic squalls, but perhaps even more political ones managed to maintain a fairly solid hold on Parliament and the electorate. It was followed by a number of Labour governments with varying majorities – an extremely feeble one to start with – but with programmes which carried a strongly reforming message and intention. Nevertheless, although the period was far from free of sometimes grave economic problems, including low growth and 'stop-go', it has seemed to many – at least in retrospect – to have been somewhat calmer than either the first post-war years that preceded it or the subsequent turbulent two decades which followed. While I would not wholly describe it, or even the greater part of it, as a 'golden age', it is understandable that many economists should have christened it thus, particularly many of those who were actively involved in the machinery of economic management.

I set out below some of the more specific reasons for this view, but in order not to get carried away by the enthusiasm these may provoke, it is well to bear in mind some less favourable facts. For example, one figure is worth quoting which is very much in line with the general thesis of relative economic decline. The annual average compound rate of growth of output between 1950 and 1973 was 2.5 per cent in Britain, with only the United States at

2.2 per cent lower in a list that covers seven industrial countries and shows Japan at 8.4 per cent at the head, followed by Germany at 5.0 per cent, Italy at 4.8, France at 4.2 and Canada at 3.0.

Other signs of relative under-performance are even clearer when we compare the latter part of the period. Between 1957 and 1967 the rate of growth of the UK's GDP was only 65 per cent of the average rate for the members of the OECD. It was little more than half of that of France and Germany, and one-third of that of Japan. It was even below that of the United States, which was then experiencing a period of slow growth. The *per capita* figure in real terms for the UK was in that period still higher than those for Italy and Japan, but below those for the United States, Germany and France.

One fact to bear in mind is that the general world economic environment during this period was with few interruptions relatively favourable and encouraged the hope that at last the post-war world, with its new inter-governmental institutions, its new economic ideas and practical experiments in economic management had found the long-sought secret of sustainable growth and, broadly, avoidance of inflationary and deflationary sways. The Bretton Woods institutions were at last beginning to make an active impact: the World Bank on the Third World, for which it had really been created, and the IMF through the development of technically (and diplomatically) more effective programmes for assisting countries in temporary payments difficulties and for reforming the underlying causes of these.

All this naturally created a more optimistic background for the British economy. It is perhaps particularly noteworthy that the machinery of economic management as it had emerged from the first post-war Labour government was left relatively unchanged for some time by the incoming Conservative administration. The Economic Section of the Cabinet Office, which had acquired considerable status during the war as a source of analytical input into policy making, and had even enhanced it during the first Labour government, worked very closely with

23

the Economic Planning Staff created by that government and located first in the Cabinet Office and then in the Treasury. And even the Treasury, despite frequent doctrinal and practical disagreements, fundamentally worked well with them. Whether this was mainly due to the happy accident that there was close personal co-operation at the top of these institutions, or to a convergence of diagnoses of the country's ills and of the possible solutions available is difficult to say but not really relevant. A further factor was that there was a relatively easy relationship between many Ministers and both old and temporary officials due partly to their not dissimilar backgrounds and similar wartime experiences. At any rate, it is not surprising that many economists who actively worked in the 'machine' at the time should look back upon it as a specially productive period.

The general operation of Whitehall departments also remained for a time remarkably similar to what it had been with even the Planning Board an integral part of the machinery. On the policy front, there was, of course, some change of emphasis. The new ruling party was generally reluctant to continue what they regarded as Labour-inspired controls, state intervention generally, the strong position of the trade unions and high taxation. Indeed, these sentiments were widely enough shared to have brought the party to victory. But in their commitment to full employment, growth, some improvement of living standards and maintenance of the welfare state the position of the new government was not greatly different from that of the old.

I have already shown that a highly optimistic view of this phase is revealed as somewhat superficial when the British economy is compared not only with the United States or Japan, already showing signs of growing into an economic giant, but with a number of continental countries.

What is also particularly noteworthy is that all this took place when the government had political problems to deal with that were even more difficult than the Korean War. This war with all its strains, particularly on human resources, had also opened up to the Attlee government the prospect of what seemed to be a new lease of life of the special relationship, but it was soon shown to be illusory. The political problems, which related to the rapidly increasing pressure for the transformation or abolition of old colonial and similar bonds preoccupied some Ministers, including the Prime Minister, up to 1958. Winston Churchill, enfeebled by a stroke, and Anthony Eden, first as Foreign Secretary, then as Prime Minister, were uninterested in economic problems. The latter was totally absorbed by the Suez crisis following the invasion of Egypt – a rare example, alas in a totally misguided direction, of close Anglo-French co-operation.

From the viewpoint of today it looks almost as if there was a separation within the government between concern with the post-war, post-imperial international political world pattern and the adaptation of Britain's position to it, and the management of the economic problems which continued to be pressing. If ever Adam Smith's advice, quoted at the head of this section, was relevant it was during this period; significantly, it had been given by him in direct relation to a similar major turnaround, the fate of the American colonies. Not surprisingly, an appreciation of this kind of consideration was more present in the minds of officials in the Treasury and the various economic advisers than at the top of government. It can therefore be said of the most general level of economic management that one of the major errors of policy in the 1950s and early 1960s was a gross over-estimation of the resources we had to meet all the domestic and international claims. Generally, the choices were made to the detriment of the former.

Once again, balance of payments problems were the clearest symptom of this excessive burden. There was continuing pressure on reserves and the exchange rate resulting from the precarious balance of payments situation, the foundations for which had already been laid earlier. It is not necessary to trace here in detail the occasions when these showed up in critical form. In outline, the exchange rate was under special pressure in 1955, and a monetary squeeze was designed to meet this situation. There was a fiscal squeeze later that year. In 1957 and 1958 a further effort was made by monetary and fiscal means to cope with inflation and, thus, indirectly the external problem. All these were repeated with monotonous regularity up to the disappearance of the Conservative government in 1964, leaving behind for the Labour government that followed, which had a bare majority, the largest balance of payments deficit yet.

ROBOT

One particular policy effort during this period that deserves special mention is the proposal worked out by two Treasury officials, Sir Leslie Rowan and Sir Richard (Otto) Clarke, and one from the Bank of England, Sir George Bolton, to make sterling fully convertible but at a floating exchange rate. This would allow, as it was put at the time, the exchange rate rather than the reserves 'to take the strain' of the balance of payments fluctuations. The plan, known as ROBOT, composed from the syllables of the authors' names, but also thought to illustrate to perfection the nature and *modus operandi* of the proposed mechanism, though it was never adopted and is old history now, is worth mention for two reasons. Firstly, it illustrates perfectly the dilemma of policy choices and the fact that these were essentially addressed to symptoms rather than to underlying causes; and secondly, because it is important to decide whether or not its rejection was a major policy error.

It is not necessary to go into the technical arguments that were deployed on both sides of the debate, which seems mainly to have been about the likely future course of the exchange rate once floated and the effect on financial markets as well as on our obligations, legal and moral, to the world's monetary system. The debate was not so much concerned with the more distant and deeper macro-economic consequences, some similar, some different from those of a straightforward devaluation. The three authors' advocacy was countered by powerful arguments from the government's chief planner, Sir Edwin (now Lord) Plowden, and chief economist, Sir Robert Hall, and from the personal adviser to the Prime Minister, Lord Cherwell. With the final successful persuasion of the Foreign Secretary, Anthony Eden, of whom it can be said without any offence that he did not understand the argument, the latter won the day. One thing is certain, this great battle cannot be said to have been decided on the merits – if indeed this is at all inherently possible in a matter of this kind. It was decided by a typical gladiatorial contest for the ear of those with ultimate power to decide, who are more often than not the ones least versed in the substance of the argument.

Was it perhaps the greatest policy error of the post-war period, as Otto Clarke maintained to the end of his life? Would it have freed us at a stroke from the incubus of the balance of payments constraints and enabled us to pursue more rational domestic policies? Would it have made it impossible to avoid a more stringent use of resources, particularly for external purposes, than was in fact done? And does the experience of subsequent periods of floating or devaluing sterling support this thesis?

It is of course impossible to prove these propositions or their opposites. It can however be said that the plan had a boldness which was singularly lacking in nearly all the policy decisions – except, as we shall see, the fatal, negative one in relation to European integration.

To answer the questions posed above, it is neither necessary nor possible to go over the arguments at the time. I believe that the only one the authors found it impossible to get round was the near-certainty of adverse reaction by the Commonwealth, because a large part of the sterling balances were to be blocked; by the United States because, notwithstanding convertibility, floating would have offended certain principles of world monetary arrangements held dear by the Americans; and probably by the Europeans, who would not have gone along with one variant of the plan, namely to present it as a collective European approach to convertibility. It was no doubt the virtual certainty of this foreign storm occurring which must have weighed with the Foreign Secretary and the Prime Minister, in so far as he was then able to judge.

27

Leaving on one side this almost certainly decisive factor, I would now say that the decision to turn down ROBOT was an error. Certainly it required a plunge into the unknown, but one has only to remember the subsequent course of events to the very end of the Conservative government and right through the six years of subsequent Labour government to see that a bold new move would have been preferable. The period contained perennial exchange/reserves/balance of payments crises, relieved by re-course to the IMF as well as by direct borrowings in markets when possible and from foreign central banks and treasuries. And all these crises were accompanied by recurrent debates about devaluation and some actual ones.

Labour in Office

In 1964 Labour again came to power with an exiguous majority which it was to enlarge to a more comfortable margin two years later. This government inherited a record balance of payments deficit that was not only the result of several years of general neglect of the underlying causes and of mainly symptomatic therapy but also of the so-called 'dash for growth' of the last year or so of the preceding government.

It is fair to say that the election victory found the party not only unprepared for what 'the books' revealed (which they not unnaturally made much of) but also, after twelve years, relatively unprepared for the practices of government, since few of the new Ministers had had any previous experience. It also suffered from the after-effects of a sharp leadership struggle after the death of Hugh Gaitskell, the scars of which were a continuing irritation thereafter. This combination proved to be a difficult one when it was applied to the pressing immediate problem. Nevertheless, under the slogan of 'getting Britain going again' after what had certainly been a somewhat stagnant period, the government showed at any rate a readiness to try new methods.

Of institutional innovations, I mention the creation of regional councils, the intensification of the activities of the tripartite

National Economic Development Council and the setting up of a series of 'little Neddies', i.e. sectoral or functional committees under the Council, and a general attempt to create a co-operative atmosphere between government, the employers (under the Confederation of British Industry, as it came to be called at a later stage) and the trade unions. The arrangements for providing the government with economic advice were changed where this was consequential upon the institution of the new Department of Economic Affairs; but this was perhaps less substantive than mechanical. Possibly more important were certain changes in personnel which brought into the immediate entourage of Ministers, and particularly the Prime Minister, economists and others more in tune with Ministers' own views. In this respect, the situation was significantly different from that of the 1952 Conservative government, which seemed to be less sensitive regarding the opinions and attitudes of their advisers.

The broad lines of economic policy which the government was attempting to follow were in many respects remarkably daring considering the government's precarious parliamentary position. This applied not only to established instruments, such as fiscal policy, where major changes in the level and structure of taxation were introduced (income tax, capital gains and corporation tax as well as indirect taxation – at a later stage the notorious Selective Employment Tax), but also to new forms of government concern with the 'real' economy, grouped under 'industrial policy', 'regional policy' and, above all, 'incomes policy'.

After twelve years in the wilderness, and with a most precarious parliamentary situation, it is understandable that the government wished to create the impression of novelty, vigour, energy and ceaseless activity. To this end they subjected the populace to such phrases as the '100 days', or the application of 'white-hot' technology or the apparently far-reaching institutional changes of which the new Department of Economic Affairs was the example. Most of their broad-ranging policies, on the other hand, could only be effective in the long term.

Novelty was also forced on the government by the alarming state of sterling, and therefore of the reserves. These were under tremendous pressure, owing to the usual self-accelerating loss of confidence in markets, and the scepticism, not to say hostility, with which some of the government's taxation and other policies, including the continued commitment to nationalization, were received by the financial communities at home and abroad (the 'gnomes of Zurich'). The avowed intention to nationalize large parts of the banking system – the clearing banks and at least one merchant bank – as well as the steel industry was not calculated to reassure opinion. While the bark in this regard turned out to be worse than the bite, doubt had been created. In fact, in this area, the main innovation turned out to be the creation of a kind of government-controlled merchant bank, the Industrial Reconstruction Corporation, which, though not very welcomed by the City, carried on for some years relatively undisturbed as an additional part of the departmental machine. It was not significantly successful in any innovative, initiating sense.

The all-embracing policy of the government, which was supposed to fuse all the individual parts into a more powerful whole, was the 'Plan'. Inspired to a large extent by French precedent, it eschewed direction and command, though in fact these continued here and there outside the framework of the Plan itself. Instead, the Plan relied on setting out targets in various areas for some years ahead and drawing up lists of actions which different sections of society and the economy were exhorted to take in order to reach the stated objectives.

This system, if it can be called that, was underpinned by the entire apparatus of formal or informal tripartite discussion and consultation together with specific 'sorties' by individual Ministers or the Prime Minister to stimulate or rescue sections of industry or individual firms. The sum total of all these efforts certainly had a degree of logical consistency, though this was not evident at the outset. A strictly centrally directed Plan, the longing of the left wing of the party, was out, and even on the subject of nationalization there was sharp division which in practice resulted in the virtual abandonment of a long-cherished principle. Moreover, given the existence of many other instruments for influencing the private sector (at a time when the private sector was still strongly habituated to close contact with government wishes), the whole apparatus might have been made to work for a while.

A further most important policy strand of the Labour government, which significantly carried the whole process into the area of macro-economic management, was the attempt to revive and strengthen incomes policy. Indeed, it is no exaggeration to say that the main energy of the new Department of Economic Affairs was directed to that end after a relatively short time. The start of the government's policy was a voluntary agreement to a solemn pledge (soon christened 'Solomon Binding') by what in other countries would be called the 'social partners', but it soon became, from an economic management point of view, the cornerstone of it. It was quickly underpinned by statutory powers, and it had for reasons of political acceptability to be accompanied by restrictions on profits and dividends. However, final success evaded this government as it had done others. The problem of how to build wage restraint into a non-inflationary growth economy was to go on reappearing periodically in our history.

That the government was not wholly committed to policies which bore a traditional Labour 'left-wing' stamp is shown by its earliest policy statement, a White Paper (soon christened the 'Brown' paper because of the apparent influence of the First Secretary, George Brown) issued within a few weeks of the government coming into power. It contained revenue raising and expenditure cutting measures (also accompanied by monetary stringency) of an impeccably 'orthodox' kind.

Europe was not, during this period, as acute an issue as it had been when the Conservatives were still in power, and the Brussels negotiations plus the immediate *sequelae* of their failure were not uppermost on the political agenda. The new government was at least spared for a time the difficulty of taking an overt position; and in any event a resumption of negotiations was not yet practical politics. Inside Whitehall and within the governing party debate continued. The earlier attitude of the Labour Party was divided, but on balance hostile to the Community. Those in favour were certainly not willing to take any major risks to change this view. The departed leader, Hugh Gaitskell, had, surprisingly, been strongly hostile. The reasons can only be speculated on now, but they stemmed from an amalgam of mental attitudes formed over many years: a pre-war experience of the fate of social democracy in Central Europe at the hands of Nazism, not very rationally leading to suspicion of the continental leaders of the integration movement as being Catholic, right-wing, economically on the whole *laissez-faire* and anti-planning. Although by no means anti-American, the support for European integration by the United States had the opposite effect on him. Above all, perhaps, a strong attachment to the Commonwealth, particularly India, made him fearful of the economic as well as political consequences of Britain being absorbed into the new Europe.

His attitude, despite the considerable authority he enjoyed (not only in his own party) would not have been enough to determine the whole stance of the party to the problem, but it happened to make a natural complement to the trade unions' fears of a movement apparently dominated by right-wing parties, as well as of those sections of the whole Labour movement who still saw economic salvation in the creation of a planned economy. The government that came into power after Gaitskell's death was not so definitely committed against the Community – indeed it contained a number of strongly pro-Europe Ministers – but since there was no obvious outside pressure to become more active in this area, and since domestic problems were all-absorbing, nothing much was done – except in the usual study-ing, discussing and paper writing activities of Whitehall – until after the re-election of the government with a larger majority in 1966.

Devalue or Not?

In the meantime, the recurring, and in some respects worsening, economic problems had greatly weakened the prospects of a successful resumption of the European negotiations, both as regards the self-confidence of the potential British negotiators as well as the receptivity of the Six, notably the French. This is particularly seen in the meeting between some leading British and French Ministers and a small official team in the summer of 1966 which came to nothing despite an apparently more welcoming attitude on the French side and an almost decided readiness towards membership on the British.

However, as far as willingness to become a member of the Community is concerned, it would not be fair to put the blame at the door of the British government on this occasion. One of the main obstacles proved once again to be the precarious state of sterling. In fact, the position of sterling, of the reserves and of the balance of payments had presented virtually a continuous crisis during the first two years of the government, and continued to do so up to the end of the decade, though in less acute form after the devaluation of 1967. If possible errors of policy are to be examined, it is in this area that we have to probe. Faced with the balance of payments problem bequeathed to it by its predecessor, and with the consequent critical moves of the exchange rate and the reserves (bulletins on these being circulated at short intervals to some Ministers and officials as on the state of a critically ill patient) one of the earliest choices the government had to make was whether to devalue or not.

Devaluation was supported, though not very vociferously, by some Ministers and by most of the newly appointed advisers. It was opposed by the Prime Minister and his two principal colleagues, and by most of the most senior levels of the bureaucracy. Almost simultaneously with the decision to issue the White Paper mentioned above, the principal members of the government took the decision not to devalue, and further internal discussion

33

of this issue was discouraged. It rambled on, however, and came to the fore (within government circles, that is) in 1966 at the same time, and to some extent logically linked with, the question of resuming talks with the French and possibly later applying for membership of the Economic Community.

Much has been said and written about the negative decision in 1964, its repetition in even more draconian form in 1966, when it also carried an absolute Prime Ministerial veto on further official discussion, and the eventual collapse of this policy a year later. There are those who argued then, and would probably argue now, that the failure to devalue at the outset of the new régime, when the cause could have been 'blamed' on the predecessor government, was its gravest policy error. The economic arguments either way were not very clear then, nor are they now. Devaluation might have had a further unfavourable effect on confidence at a time when Britain was, whatever was done about the exchange rate, heavily dependent in the short run on foreign financial assistance – which was in fact forthcoming. The general state of the utilization of resources of the tendencies towards inflation and of the doubtful ability to expand exports quickly to take advantage of a more competitive exchange rate did not point to a certain advantage to be derived from devaluation.

Indeed, when the debate was resumed at a later stage much of the discussion turned on the question of whether it was more effective to 'dig a hole' first (i.e. to bring about a slack in resource use by macro-economic means) or to devalue first. What is almost certainly the case is that, apart from the balance of economic argument, Ministers were heavily influenced by the fact that folk memory of the last, 1949, devaluation would result in Labour being branded as the 'party of devaluation'.

I do not think that the omission of devaluation in 1964 was in itself a major policy error, although it would have obviated the need for some measures which had an unfavourable external effect, such as the imposition of an import surcharge, which greatly upset the EFTA partners.

The uncertainties of policy, which included varying experiments with incomes policy on a voluntary and statutory basis (which were short-lived) came to an initial halt with the Party Executive's rejection of the 1969 White Paper and a complete stop soon after with the party's loss of power. In addition, in order to stave off continuing exchange crises, there were various cosmetic measures as well as external borrowing. Policy then appeared to reach some definiteness on two related points. In July 1966, in a series of measures hotly contested inside the Cabinet, including an only temporarily withdrawn resignation by George Brown, the government 'dug' the famous hole by announcing expenditure cutbacks of £500 million at home and £150 million abroad. In May 1967 this was followed by the government applying again for membership of the European Economic Community, but in December that year this was vetoed by the French, together with applications by Ireland, Denmark and Norway.

It is pointless to attempt to categorize as erroneous any part of these and others of a series of policy initiatives which followed each other with great speed, except for the devaluation which came in November 1967. Its timing in relation to the July 1966 measures and the attempt to resume the European negotiations was such as to invalidate the arguments adduced for defending the failure to devalue in 1964, particularly given the comfortable majority the party had achieved in the 1966 election and the government's more determined attack on the fiscal front that year, as well as its changed attitude to Europe. It is not absolutely certain that if this error had been avoided, and if devaluation had been timed differently in relation to the other policies, it would have been really effective this time. The probability is, however, that it would have been. The uncertainty with which the government proceeded is shown very clearly by the fact that when the devaluation came the Prime Minister felt obliged to accompany it with the assurance that 'the pound in your pocket' had not been devalued, a statement which was a dubious piece of economics and was soon found out to be so in practice.

35

Surveying the whole of this long period, I conclude that the specific policy errors to which I have pointed are also indicative of a more general failure. For the first twelve years, no real attempt was made to grapple with the more deep-seated causes of our post-war troubles; while in the next six enthusiasm weighted with ideology battled against and was worn down by the daily political pressures inside and outside the ruling party. If external circumstances are brought into the reckoning, the mistakes of our policy makers seem understandable and excusable. The Middle East erupting into a violence which has not yet ceased; the United States having to cope with the economic burden of the Vietnam War as well as with that of the 'great society'; the increasing Soviet aggressiveness, Hungary in 1957, Czechoslovakia in 1968; the measures taken by the United States to deal with their aggravated balance of payments deficit, which transformed the landscape of international financial markets, but also caused considerable problems for some of her trading partners and renewed General de Gaulle's anti-American sentiments – all these may be adduced in our defence as extenuating circumstances. They do not, however, wipe the slate clean.

In this connection it is significant that in the latter part of this period – the late 1960s – the Washington Brookings Institution organized a team of American and Canadian economists to examine Britain's economic performance. Its report was published in 1968, and while it acknowledged that Britain's performance since the Second World War was superior to that before it, it did highlight the under-performance relative to other countries to which I have already drawn attention. The record therefore remains as stated.

The European Problem

Another highly significant and equally long-lasting example of quite inadequate appreciation of changing world events is Britain's attitude to the pressure for European integration, which assumed great strength on the 're-launching of Europe' in 1955, following the failure (in the end through French parliamentary rather than the original powerful British opposition) of the proposal for a European Defence Community. I have given a fairly detailed account of the actual course of our attempt to reach a clear policy in Europe at that time.* This was more or less finally achieved by the decision of the Macmillan Cabinet in 1961 to apply for membership under the terms of the Treaty of Rome.

The preceding period of preparation and the subsequent nearly two years of negotiation show how arduous a task it was to attempt to find the 'ideal' solution, the best of all possible worlds. Throughout, we were attempting to sail between the many threatening rocks of particular interests: our farmers, Commonwealth trade, progress on world-wide trade liberalization through GATT, our domestic economic interests, ranging from the position of sterling and London's place as an international financial centre to the requirements of a world monetary system – though at a time when the survival of the Bretton Woods system was already under some doubt. Once again, also, the respective need to accept wholeheartedly the notion of a European Community proved difficult to reconcile with the desire to preserve a special relationship with the United States, an objective which at the time was paradoxically made increasingly difficult to attain by the United States' own strong pressure on us to fit in with European desires which had already become noticeable during the Marshall Plan negotiations. When we seemed on the point of accepting the inevitable, French action again 'came to the rescue': de Gaulle's veto in 1963.

One important point to note here is that the preceding long period of hesitation, the form of the subsequent application, the negotiating briefs and postures and the actual conduct of the negotiation, which was full of special conditions and reservations, created a severe division of opinion within the country. This cut

* Eric Roll, *Crowded Hours* (Faber and Faber, 1985; reissued 1995)

across party boundaries and probably affected public opinion more profoundly than any other major policy issue had done for decades. Indeed, this situation continues to this day, though in a somewhat different form. Outside the country, those who did not want us as members were in the main Gaullists in and out of the French government. As for 'friends', as well as the Americans, who wanted us in the Community, they were numerous among the six, but they were discouraged and unable to resist de Gaulle's final opposition when it came. A lack of real foresight and a 'too little, too late' posture had, I believe, as much to do with the failure of the famous Brussels negotiations as de Gaulle's veto.

This was not, however, the end of the 'European problem'; it has dragged on to the present day. The landmark crises during these nearly thirty years clearly show a continuing thread of uncertainty as to exactly what would be the right course to take, given the need to achieve a balance between what we thought (rightly or wrongly) would suit our national interests best and what could (again rightly or wrongly) be considered attainable.

The problem is so important in itself, and so illustrative of more general uncertainties in our policy choices, that I have in what follows given a more extensive account and analysis of the considerations in regard to Europe. I have done this largely from the point of view of our dilemma *vis-à-vis* the ever-present pressure of the 'special relationship' with the United States, as it seems to me to be particularly illuminating as a guide to our predicament.

Across the Atlantic or Across the Channel?

Britain's attitude and policy in relation to the movement for European integration raises many issues that go far beyond the purely economic. The subject nevertheless needs to be discussed in connection with my general theme. In the first place, the economic component of Britain's role in Europe over my chosen period is quite considerable. Trade and financial relations with the countries on the European continent play a large part in determining the level of our economic activity. They also condition many aspects of the macro-economic environment in which we conduct our financial and industrial affairs, whether a particular aspect is formally part of an international institutional nexus or not. In short, we have always been intimately linked with most of these countries. It is therefore inevitable that when we analyze our changing economic performance we should have to ask what our relations with the major continental countries have been and how far these relations have influenced our performance.

This is all the more necessary because the strong tendency for increasing integration has in recent decades been a major dynamic force in the political and economic development of Europe. Moreover, the uncertainties and vacillations which have characterized our reaction to this tendency strongly resemble other uncertainties that may account for deficiencies in our economic performance at least since the end of the Second World War.

The 'European Question' has been a major problem for Britain, particularly in the last thirty years. Britain's attitude is best described as ambivalent, or, more harshly, equivocal. The movement for a closer union of European countries has a long history and has appeared in various forms at least throughout this century. It is, however, true to say that until the 1930s it could hardly be regarded as powerful enough to enter into the practical calculations of European statesmen. It certainly did not present British politicians or the British public in general with anything like an acute problem requiring definite and difficult economic or political choices. Nevertheless, the foundations for the dilemmas that were to plague British policy makers after the Second World War were already laid in the turbulent 1930s.

It was during this period that the rise of Fascism in Italy, and even more of Nazism in Germany, made clear to those who were prepared to look searchingly enough at these developments the extreme dangers of unbridled nationalism feeding on economic crisis and depression. From the point of view of subsequent developments of British policy, what was particularly important was that the 1930s clearly completed the process of the decline of Britain's unique position as the economic, financial and military 'super-power' – a term to be invented later. For a century or more, the world order had largely rested on the *Pax Britannica* maintained by the British Navy, which went hand in hand with an *Aequilibrium Britannicum*, managed, via the gold standard and its 'rules of the game', by the Bank of England and the City of London. The replacement of these pillars by a *Pax Americana* (managed at a later stage by the US Strategic Airforce) and an *Aequilibrium Americanum* managed by the US Treasury and the Federal Reserve System via the dollar, was perhaps not yet visible to everyone even if it was effectively already in existence. It still had to be consolidated and made universally evident after the war.

This shift in the world's power pattern added substantially to the urge of the continental countries to get closer together, an urge which the ravages of Nazism, war and occupation had so powerfully set in train. It is significant that the principal architects of the resultant movement, particularly Jean Monnet, while conscious of the great economic power of the United States and the example which its large market and united monetary system held up to the Europeans, were in no way motivated by hostility to American power and influence. It is equally significant that the leading policy makers on the other side of the Atlantic were not only not hostile to the continental integration movement, but positively encouraged it. I speak here of the leaders on both sides: of course there were those in Europe who were motivated by fear and hostility to the United States and those in America who, even when welcoming greater integration as offering the hope of avoiding future wars and American involvement, were fearful of the consequences of economic integration and the trade discrimination against the United States that it might bring.

Britain's reaction was different. She had suffered greatly in the war but had not been occupied and had emerged as the one victorious ally at the side of the United States. Therefore, although conscious of the enormously enhanced economic power of the United States, Britain was even more conscious of the need for US economic support if Europe, including Britain, was to have a chance to recover and reconstruct. To this was added a strong awareness of the vital need to keep the United States closely linked politically and militarily to Europe in the face of Soviet military might and expansionism. The existence of strong communist parties in France and Italy created the fear that the emergence of a 'third force' between the super-powers might offer an attractive alternative to continental countries and thus become a major ingredient of the European integration movement.

At the same time the United States was anxious to deal with (Western) Europe as a group, particularly in the vital economic sphere as demonstrated in the Marshall Plan. The combination of this fact, the political fragility of a number of liberated countries and the vital need for American economic support induced us to make common cause with the principal continental countries. Indeed we took the leading part in the American–European effort of economic reconstruction through the Marshall Plan. This went hand in hand with the attempt to build a wider framework for world economic recovery through the Bretton Woods institutions.

Close co-operation between the European countries under Anglo-French leadership, and between them and the United States, was thus the *leitmotiv* of the four years of the Marshall Plan and the so-called European Recovery Programme. Nevertheless, even then tensions began to appear over such issues as the form and extent of the liberalization of trade, the convertibility of currencies and the control of the public finances. Not only did continental and British ideas – and immediate necessities – clash in these matters, but also in views on the relation between world-wide reconstruction and the institutions – GATT and so on – serving them and the scope of purely European efforts. Much of the British attitude in these matters reflected a basic dilemma (in retrospect more imaginary than real) of whether the transatlantic prospect was more attractive than the cross-Channel one.

41

The real, but in the long run and for many practical purposes overrated, 'special relationship' with the United States created the single most potent source of hesitation and uncertainty in British policy for the first twenty years or so of the post-war period. The ties with the Commonwealth played for a time a similar but subsidiary role, but – perhaps paradoxically – these proved to be a less powerful and persistent obstacle to an appreciation of the power of the 'European idea'. It is to be remembered that policy making and opinion forming was still mesmerized by the concept of Britain standing at the centre of three intersecting circles: the United States, Europe and the Commonwealth. The image of three circles was perhaps a good way of describing the difficult problems of reconciling our interests, but it led us to believe that we had more influence in all the three directions than we proved able to exercise.

On the more specifically economic plane there was concern that the creation of a world-wide commercial and financial system, an objective also dear to many American policy makers, might be imperilled by concentration on purely European economic integration. Mixed with this were some more selfish concerns, such as the settlement of sterling debts and the management of the sterling area, where American interests, sometimes as narrow as the British, often ran counter. It was indeed difficult to know how best to preserve the special relationships while paying heed to more specific interests that had to be taken care of in the constantly changing situation, and in the face of very ambivalent American attitudes. This is perhaps itself enough to account for the zig-zags of British policy, always devoted no less than that of other countries to the unattainable aim of having the best of all possible worlds.

The perplexities of British policy were not to diminish even after Marshall aid had been distributed and the OEEC had settled down to its relatively routine task, leaving, as the British had wished, wider commercial and financial problems to be dealt with in other organizations, the GATT, the IMF, the World Bank. What was most important in British eyes was that these included the United States and the Commonwealth, the latter, despite greatly loosened bonds, still an important factor in British policy making.

Europe and Defence

However, two developments ensured that the British dilemma was to become even more acute: firstly, the continued pressure for European integration, and secondly, the organization of the strategic-defensive interests in the West in Nato. From the British point of view the latter seemed to present both opportunities and concerns, but tending in opposite directions; and the fact that they came to prominence at about the same time made the dilemma for Britain that much more severe. The renewed pressure for some significant forward move on the European front was once again the work of Jean Monnet.

The history of the Monnet-conceived Schumann Plan, its semi-rejection by the British at the beginning, soon to be definitive, has been much researched and written about. Here I only want to say that, since this happened under the first post-war Labour government, it brought out yet another consideration which caused the British to refuse to consider seriously the 'European choice'. Monnet's 'sector approach' to integration made him choose the unification of the two basic industries, coal and steel, as the means of removing Franco-German rivalry and thus lay the foundation of European unity and peace, while it was just these two industries, chosen for early nationalization in Britain, that were the core of the economic planning to which the Labour Party was pledged. This special aspect of the more general fear of losing sovereignty, common at the time to British parties on the right and the left, was a particularly powerful obstacle to Britain's joining in. The extension of the Monnet proposals, first to atomic energy, and later and much more

43

seriously to the whole of the participants' economies, greatly aggravated the problem.

The consolidation of the machinery for combining the military/strategic interests of the Western powers in Nato seemed to offer Britain once again the prospect of avoiding the fearful choice in favour of Europe. With her greater military strength relative to that of America's other allies, and her interests that were still world-wide, there was still the possibility of preserving the 'special relationship' within the Western alliance. The Korean War, in which Britain made a notable military contribution, was the occasion of another attempt in the same direction. The International Materials Conference set up in the wake of Prime Minister Attlee's visit to Washington seemed to offer further possibilities of the same kind in the economic field. It was short-lived; but the successive attempts to build and institutionalize the economic concerns of Nato, to the detriment, as many Americans and most Europeans feared, of the European institutions, show clearly in which direction Britain would have preferred to go. Nato, unlike the OEEC at that time, had the Americans as full members; and an expansion of Nato's economic activities against the background of powerful strategic necessities would have constituted a strong counterweight to narrower 'European' institutions.

A small episode is worth mentioning as an interesting example of the British search for a solution of its dilemma which would take account of the 'special relationship'. American and Canadian officials were confidentially informed in September 1949 of the impending British devaluation and a Tripartite Economic Council was set up. This move was greeted with great enthusiasm in London (though not in Paris), for it seemed to offer the very thing that many British policy makers wished and many French ones feared. A most senior official was sent to Washington as British representative, but the effectiveness of this new piece of machinery did not last very long, on this occasion for the happy reason that a widespread economic recovery greatly ameliorated the British economic problem and made the new machinery less relevant.

The next ten years – not quite coterminous with the twelve years of Conservative government that followed on the six first post-war years of Labour rule – showed a continuation of the problem for Britain, resulting in alternate leanings to the Atlantic or the European side. The problem of the organization of Europe could not, however, be avoided. There were some more attempts, including one major one, to enlarge the economic competence of Nato. Various measures withered on the vine, such as a degree of standardization of weapons and more elaborate ones which concerned broader aspects of economic and financial policy. The most important of these, early in the life of Nato, was the 'burden-sharing' exercise, so-called in its early Whitehall terminology. Not surprisingly it was seized on with alacrity by the British, who saw Nato, at a time when enlargement of defence programmes was a powerful necessity, but one which competed for resources with other requirements of European, particularly British, recovery, especially the expansion of exports, as possibly the central arena for the settlement of major questions of American–European economic policy.

During these ten years, the wider economic organizations, such as the World Bank and the International Monetary Fund, at last began to lead an increasingly active life. On the trade side they were supplemented – or, as some would argue, interfered with – by special agreements on certain commodities or industrial products. And with the appearance later of yet another institution, UNCTAD, the problem of the developing world began to make a greater impact. All these seem, in retrospect at least, to have produced a less agitated environment for dealing with the problem that had previously occasioned Britain's acute dilemma.

After the Treaty of Rome

However, the net effect as far as my main theme is concerned was, after 1958, to confront Britain with what its attitude should be to the European Economic Community, which had become more and more a real force to be reckoned with since the signing of the Treaty of Rome. In the years leading up to the Treaty, there is little doubt that an important element in British policy had been a genuine doubt whether this European experiment would ever succeed. There was also an uncertainty as to whether the American support for it was as wide or as deep-seated as the protagonists made out. Subsequent conflicts on specific issues between the policy of the EEC and American interests show that doubts about the extent to which American opinion – and government policy – would be prepared to tolerate economic discrimination in the interest of a political concept – European unity – were not entirely misplaced, even if, in the end, they turned out not to justify Britain's doubts.

The history of British attempts to find some way out of the difficulty created by the undoubtedly widely held favourable view of European integration within and outside the 'Six' gave rise to many highly ingenious plans. Some of the best minds in Whitehall and some of the most skilled negotiators were enlisted in the task, firstly of creating the European Free Trade Area, and then of finding some *modus vivendi* between it and the EEC. Ostensibly, the main problem for them was to determine what Britain's relation to the rest of Western Europe should be in the economic field, but inevitably, as it seemed to many in Britain, in Europe and in the United States, the question of political relations came to predominate. The other horn of the British dilemma, the American relationship, was somewhat less in evidence, although the discriminating trade aspects of the EFTA were by no means welcome to the United States since EFTA lacked the counter-attraction of the political dimension of the EEC.

In the end it became clear to British Ministers and officials that a reconciliation between the relatively loose arrangements of EFTA and the tight domestic and external commercial policy provisions of the EEC was impossible. Moreover, it was also clear that the problems of agriculture, both in its domestic aspects, and even more in its relation to trade with the Commonwealth, would become more acute with the development of the Community and its agricultural policy.

Thus, by the beginning of the 1960s, the stage was set for a re-examination of British policy. The decision to apply for membership, the subsequent negotiations and the veto by de Gaulle at the beginning of 1963 are part of well-known history, one in which the European/American dilemma of British policy perhaps played a less crucial part. It is, however, worth considering whether the decision of 1962 itself throws any light on the British dilemma. It is worth mentioning that it marked the fulfilment of Monnet's prophecy that the British, being realists, would want to join when they saw that the Community was a working reality. So, does the decision mean that at that point Britain decided in favour of the cross-Channel prospect? Or was she merely bowing to the inevitable? In my view, it was neither wholly one nor the other, though, as always in these matters, the second contains more of the truth: immediate necessity, however perceived, will generally take precedence over broader, longer term, objectives. Of course, Ministers and advisers were motivated not only by the success – as far as it went – of the EEC, but by a fairly strong belief in the need for (or the inevitability of) European unity and the desire that Britain should participate in its creation. But many Ministers and advisers remained strongly attached not only to the Atlantic Alliance as such but more specifically to the closest possible relations with the principal ally.

I believe that it would be wrong to regard the application for EEC membership as being the result of a decisive move in the direction of a 'European choice'. It was probably the result of an almost paradoxical blend of recognition of what Adam Smith had called 'the mediocrity' of Britain's circumstances with a heightened sense of the need to strengthen Europe. At the same time there seemed also to have been a much greater degree of self-confidence by Britain in her ability to handle the intricate relationships with Europe and the United States – something which should have been more in evidence and would have been more realistic at the end of the war. A combination of these factors can account for Britain's readiness to enter into European negotiations and her confidence that the American relationship need not thereby suffer. That last aspect was clearly of special importance in the Anglo-American Nassau Agreement over nuclear weapons, which some analysts have made responsible for the de Gaulle veto.

The end of the first serious attempt to make common cause with the European economic unification movement coincided with a fresh outbreak of specifically British economic difficulties, highlighted, as so often in the period, by the severe balance of payments crisis that greeted the incoming third post-war Labour administration, just elected with a minute majority. The situation was hardly propitious for an early renewal of the attempt to join the EEC, even if the party in power had been basically more in favour of the move than it had up to that point shown itself to be. Not only did it have as its primary, indeed its overwhelming task, to cope with the immediate crisis and all that that seemed to require in novel experiments of economic and financial policy, but that task itself made dependence on American assistance, and reliance on international agencies, particularly the IMF, vital.

Ideologically, the Labour Party was not more disposed towards cleaving to America than to Europe, even though it was somewhat more sympathetic to the general thrust of the Johnson administration than to that of de Gaulle, and later, of Georges Pompidou. However, what counted was American support in overcoming the economic difficulties. Thus, any urgency that the previous government had felt about getting to terms with the EEC had greatly diminished.

Member at Last

In the broadest sense, the six years of Labour government were a period during which the American/European dilemma was at its least acute in terms of actual governmental preoccupation. It received a new impetus in 1970 with the arrival at the helm of

Edward Heath, the man who had been the first principal negotiator for entry into Europe. As far as economic policy was concerned, he tried, particularly in the early days of his administration, to orient it towards a more liberal course. This, at least as far as British–European trade relations were concerned, seemed more in harmony with the essential principles of Community policy.

The first thing to note is that in the intervening period the world had changed: in particular the economic supremacy of the United States seemed no longer completely assured, and the world financial system was on the point of breaking down. With hindsight, both factors should have made it easier for Britain to adopt a more positive attitude towards Europe. It was, in fact, made more difficult by our own continuing economic weakness, particularly the acute financial problems of 1976, and the gradual erosion of the standing and of the self-confidence of Labour governments. Later on, the weakness was accompanied by internal dissensions in the Conservative Party, culminating in a dramatic change of leadership.

So, in 1973, nine years after de Gaulle's veto we became members of the European Economic Community. Did our new-gained membership mean the end of the dilemma in relation to the United States? The history of the first seven years of British membership does not throw much light on the question, though it contained two more years of Conservative government and five years of Labour with a change of Prime Minister half-way through. There were many new occasions for disputes between Britain and the other members, new as well as old, notably on the working of the common agricultural policy and the financial arrangements within the Community, but there is no evidence that I can see that the triangular problem, i.e. the relationship with the USA, played a consistently significant part in British policy during this period.

There were of course instances, particularly in the financial sphere and in the aftermath of the breakdown of the Bretton Woods system and the successive oil shocks of the 1970s, when

Britain, having preserved in one respect particularly a certain independence of action by refusing to become a full member of the European Monetary System would sometimes 'line up' with the USA, and sometimes make common cause with one or other of its European partners. It is, however, not possible, in my view, to derive any definite conclusion either way about the triangular problem, especially as the matter is blurred on the one hand by the growing economic importance of Japan during this period, and on the other by the variations in the attitudes of some of the other EEC members, particularly Germany. Furthermore, and this may be a very important continuing feature, American interest in the development of the EEC was becoming less intense. The 'grand design' of the 1960s had disappeared from the centre of the stage.

Although the hankering after a meaningful special relationship did not disappear, it certainly played a less decisive role in our attitude to our partners in the European Community. For other reasons, however, our attitude to the development of the Community continued to be ambivalent. The Conservative government that came into power in 1979 under Margaret Thatcher certainly soon showed its own ambivalence – most strongly in an increasing discrepancy between a broad rhetoric that veered sharply from pro- to anti-European and a practical attitude to particular European initiatives.

The early signs of ambivalence were in relation to matters which could be presented as practical issues calling for defence of national interests that were not only legitimate in themselves but could be related to relatively simple financial choices. Thus, the fierce battles over the Community's budget and our contribution to it could be presented in a way that commanded much support in Parliament and the press, even though they disrupted relations with the Community's institutions and with many of our individual partners at a time when our *bona fides* towards the basic concepts of the Community was by no means solidly established.

These difficulties with our partners soon became more significant, as the close co-operation between France and Germany – in many respects, the cornerstone of the Community – took a further upward turn under Schmidt and Giscard. And at the same time, with Roy Jenkins President of the Commission, the Community was preparing to jettison its earlier monetary experiment of the 'snake' and to adopt the European Monetary System in 1979.

The Community Moves Forward

This proved to be the single most important development, if not since the Treaty of Rome, then certainly since the enlargement of the Community in the 1970s. The fact that we did not join the operative part of the system – the Exchange Rate Mechanism – served to increase and intensify the feeling of our partners that our attitude was fundamentally different from theirs, and that our strong reservations about the very purpose and destiny of the Community continued to operate, whatever our response, which was sometimes very positive in appearance, to individual plans and actions.

Occasionally major speeches by Ministers belied even this appearance of support, such as the notorious Bruges speech with its cheaply demagogic charge that 'Europeans' wished to create an 'identikit European'. It is impossible to judge whether those politicians in both the major parties who most clearly demonstrated this basic hostility genuinely represented the essence of British public opinion as some of them claimed. Their attitude was influential enough to leave a lasting impression on our continental partners, and on interested parties everywhere, which served to undermine, not only within the Community but in the world at large, the effectiveness of what officially appeared as our European policy.

In the most recent phases of Community history, this ambiguity in our behaviour has also extended into fields other than the economic. Under the pressure of external events, notably a totally changed strategic and economic map of Central and

Eastern Europe, new questions concerning the foreign policy and defence posture and activity of the Community have come to the fore. Once again Britain's position remains ambiguous. It combines a tenacious clinging to Nato, in itself defensible, with a moderate leaning towards an already existing, but not hitherto very potent Western European Union and a sometimes strong, sometimes muted, opposition to any new incursion of the Community into diplomatic or strategic areas.

Yet at the same time no opportunity is lost by the so-called Euro-sceptics of accusing the Community of paralysis or at least ineffectiveness, for example, in regard to the tragic and highly dangerous developments in what remains of Yugoslavia. This kind of double talk is not unknown elsewhere and is indeed the inevitable small change of politicians' discourse. In the British case, however, it serves to highlight still further what seems to be a fundamentally hostile attitude to Europe.

The singling out of our policy towards 'Europe' as one of the main dubious elements of our post-war position does not mean that policy in other respects of foreign relations was always free from error or that debate over this or that aspect of European policy at this or that stage was, and is, not justified. It is also true, however, that successes were more frequent in some areas. Perhaps the outstanding example is the manner in which many old imperial ties were transformed or dissolved without lasting damage.

Our policy towards the European Community is moreover central to many other vital areas of policy, spanning economic and financial matters as well as broader issues of foreign policy towards the rest of the world.

A Change of Course and Back Again, 1971–9

The next ten years of this story again saw an alternation of Conservative and Labour governments, the former under Edward Heath. It was succeeded by a Labour administration which lasted from 1974 to 1979, when the Conservatives again took over, forming an administration which has lasted until the present day.

There had been signs, perhaps more obvious now than they were at the time, that the economic situation was improving, especially so far as the perennial balance of payments problem was concerned. This was decisively so when a surplus at last appeared towards the end of 1969, at which time restrictive policies to save foreign exchange were somewhat eased though not radically changed. This improvement was, however, not enough to save the Labour government, especially as an election was pending. In that mysterious manner which even those who are most intimately involved cannot quite explain, the government had 'run out of steam'. The inability over such a long time, and for a Labour government especially, to cope with the problem of integrating trade union attitudes and actions into the politico-economic apparatus was probably the main cause of disintegration.

Somewhat surprisingly, the Conservative government that followed did not make this issue a major plank in its platform as was to happen nearly a decade later. The main new thrust bore in many respects a curious similarity to that of the 1964 Labour government. 'To change the course of history of this nation' was the slogan of the incoming Prime Minister. The task was to infuse a new spirit of enterprise, and particularly technological innovation, into the economy, though, of course, this time with the emphasis on individual private effort rather than on that of the state.

In this regard, the government started an ideological movement which was to come to full flower at the end of the decade, though in contrast to what was to come later there was little harking back to the beauties of Adam Smith's market, governed by the 'invisible hand'. A more pragmatic distinction between the activities which the state could and could not be expected to carry out efficiently was the main consideration. In addition, the government machine, where it was thought to be necessary, would have to be made more efficient and more 'cost-effective', a phrase which had become fashionable.

Again, not too different from some aspects of Labour rhetoric of six years earlier, there was much talk of improving the private enterprise machinery itself, particularly in regard to finance for industry. Here the close involvement of the German and French banks in funding industrial development, and their staffs with industrial experience, including technical and engineering, was contrasted with the attitudes, practices and lack of expert knowledge of British banks. This was a highly debatable proposition and certainly ignored the very different history of the machinery of capital formation in Britain and the Continent; but more important it directed the attention of Ministers to objectives which were either wrong or unattainable in the short term. While the administrative and advisory apparatus was not the object of suspicion by the new government that it had been on earlier occasions, and was very markedly to be again later, there was some sign of it, although this did not have a significant effect. Nor were there major changes in the organization of the machinery of government despite some preoccupation in this regard by the leaders of the victorious party before the election.

In any event, the enthusiasm and energy of the first two years of the new government were, as far as the economy was concerned, dampened by a somewhat deteriorating situation. The current balance of payments surplus began to diminish until it appeared only just adequate to meet immediate future requirements, including debt repayment. Growth also turned out to be less buoyant than expected. What was more important, both in its early economic effects and as a foretaste of what was to prove fatal in the end, was the wages explosion. In the first year of the government, 1970, the percentage rise in wages was more than twice as great as it had been in the previous period. This affected prices, though not to the same extent. Over the next twelve months the government appears to have increased its attention to this problem, both as far as how to deal with the trade unions was concerned and what to do with the inflationary consequences of 'wage push'. A whole series of specific measures that were partly inspired by the inflationary danger, but more at this stage by the general ideological commitment of the government, resulted in the dismantling of many survivals of an earlier epoch. These ranged from the abolition of the Labour-created Board for Prices and Incomes, a part of the machinery to deal with incomes policy, to the shift from investment grants to tax allowances.

More directly relevant was the attitude to wage bargaining. While the government was, as was to be expected, anxious to shift responsibility to the individual enterprise and its workforce, it could not divest itself of direct involvement in the very important large public sector. The first very active phase of public sector wage demands, sometimes backed by strikes or the threat of strikes, showed the government determined to put a brake on what was rightly regarded as excessive and an economically dangerous tendency. At the same time, by not denigrating the whole machinery of negotiation, including the use of committees and courts of enquiry, the government was able to preserve a relatively effective practice of dialogue with the unions. This situation was short-lived. It deteriorated during the remainder of the government's life to 1976 and was to become very different a few years later.

The reforming zeal of the government, less rhetorical and more substantial than it often is, lacked real effectiveness and much of it ran into the sands. It proved incapable of coming to terms with the problem of inflation, the related question of fiscal policy and consequently policy *vis-à-vis* the trade unions. There was a good deal of uncertainty in intellectual analysis and execution, and, as we shall see shortly, this combined with some external shocks to bring the government down.

However, one move can be put on the credit side, the resumption and eventual solution of the immediate European problem. As de Gaulle had forecast, it was under the leadership of the first negotiator, Edward Heath, that, this time, the British application for membership was successful; and on 1 January 1973 Britain became a member of the Community. Neither Parliament nor the country can be said to have been united behind this move, but a majority was; and that was enough to heal temporarily, though not completely, a rift between Britain and its continental neighbours that had lasted twenty years.

If one looks for reasons that brought about this change, they can be found in two facts that had at last been borne in on British policy makers. The first was that the Community, contrary to many expectations (and some hopes!) was still there and functioning reasonably well fifteen years after it had started; and that it seemed to have brought some benefit to its members. The second was the inescapable intractability of our own economic problems – on the basis of our standing alone – in world trade and finance, notwithstanding our continuing and not negligible strength in the Commonwealth, the United States and much of the Third World. Even before we had become members, our trade with members of the Community had proved to be the most buoyant and growing part of our international trade. In addition to a broader appreciation of what European integration did, and could, mean in the minds of many, particularly the Prime Minister, these two facts were a solid enough foundation on which to base a realistic change of course.

Membership did not, however, bring any immediate tangible results, and the government had to go on coping with the problems of our own economy, which, notwithstanding the substantial new oil and gas resources, was gravely affected by world events. The economy was plagued by the simultaneous rise and aggravation of the twin problems of unemployment and inflation, the 'stagflation' that was to become a frequent new phenomenon not only in Britain but world-wide. The government's policy response was not able to defeat decisively either one or the other of these, let alone both. Fiscal and monetary stimuli for one of the problems only aggravated the other; nor did policy makers, including the advisers, seem clear either about the effect of unemployment on wage claims or, if the effect could be clearly foreseen (which it could not) what policy to choose as being both effective and politically realistic.

The problem was aggravated by what was happening beyond our borders. There were seismic shocks during the critical period when the government was beset by severe problems of controlling the domestic economy that made this task almost impossible. These were the weakening of the world's monetary system as established at Bretton Woods between 1971 and 1973, when it collapsed as the result of America's suspension of convertibility; the rise of world raw material prices between 1972 and 1974, which nullified earlier improvements in Britain's terms of trade; and the oil shocks between 1971 and 1974, which ended up by quintupling the price of crude oil. This affected the situation indirectly, because it was world-wide, but also directly, notwithstanding Britain's North Sea position.

Even if these factors are called in to explain and excuse Britain's deteriorating performance during the first half of the 1970s, this cannot be a complete answer. A second study of Britain's economic performance up to roughly the end of the decade by the Brookings Institution indicts other factors for Britain's inadequate adaptability to these external shocks: defects in the labour market; industrial organization; the capital market; the educational system; and other aspects of British society.

At this stage, and in terms of the problem the government had to cope with up to its demise in 1974, the labour market problem, i.e. wage settlements, and industrial relations generally were the most immediate and powerful. It seemed impossible to find the right combination of fiscal and monetary policy to prevent a deterioration of growth and employment, while at the same time not only dealing with current wage pressures but also reforming the statutory basis of industrial relations, to which the government was committed. In fact, policy seemed to go in opposite directions and thus aggravate the tensions. The government seemed determined not to abandon reflationary policies, particularly since their first effects had been a fall in unemployment (by the end of 1973 to half a million). Since the government was also committed to reducing public expenditure, the reflationary stimulus had to come on the side of taxation. This is in fact

57

what happened. Expansion was still the watchword and when the inhibition on it on the side of the exchange rate was lifted by the floating of the pound with an immediate devaluation of 7 per cent, the way was clear for the full flowering of what came to be known as the 'Barber boom'.

A way to counter inflation other than by fiscal means had therefore to be found, and once more 'incomes policy' was turned to. An attempt to revive some sort of informal tripartite machinery ran up against the antagonism of the unions, which had been created by the new Industrial Relations Act, though this proved powerless when put to the test in connection with a claim by the railway unions. It is unnecessary here to go through all the various incidents of wage claims, attempts to reach agreement on machinery and methods between the CBI and TUC independently of government or of the government's own negotiations with the unions concerning a possible repeal of the Industrial Relations Act. In a curious way the period seems reminiscent of those hectic early days of the 1964 Labour government with often a similar institutional cast, e.g. the NEDC, but with different personalities.

When the attempt to bring about effective voluntary machinery finally failed towards the end of 1972, the government attempted to resort to a statutory incomes policy (again highly reminiscent of what had happened before), which began with a prices and wages freeze, a policy that had been tried in a number of countries and had never been successful for more than a very short period. The 1973 'neutral' budget was nevertheless still reflationary and designed to stimulate growth since there were signs of expanding economic activity.

The last few months of the government saw many of the earlier difficulties reach critical dimensions. Oil prices were three times their original level, and on the industrial relations front, action against the statutory incomes policy by the electrical workers and, in a more intensive form, by the miners reached a stage when the government's continued existence became jeopardized. It is not necessary to describe the details of these few

58

months when the confrontation between government and the organized labour movement reached a pitch which had not been experienced for many years, one highlighted by the three-day week which started on 1 January 1974. Severe cuts in public expenditure and increases in taxation finally heralded a complete reversal of the previous policy mix. In retrospect it appears that there were fleeting moments during that short period when some getting together of more moderate elements in the trade unions and of Ministers who were thought still to be amenable to a reconciliation might have avoided what looked like a virtual breakdown of organized government. However, some elements on both sides continued to be intransigent, and in the end the government was obliged to go to the country and to accept defeat at the polls.

It is not possible to run through this very summarized recital of government policies without concluding that they were erroneous. Admittedly, external circumstances were not propitious, indeed they were at times gravely complicating. Admittedly also, the history of attempts to reach accommodation with the trade union movement in regard to their conduct in relation to the changes in the macro-economic situation, under both Labour and Conservative governments, was far from encouraging. Nevertheless, it is hard to escape the conclusion that policy was vacillating between attempts at a consensus and unilateral, including statutory, measures that were a complicated mixture of dealing with the immediate situation and finding a long-term reform. Both sides vacillated between intransigence and readiness to seek agreement. The unions demonstrated, as did the government, a failure to look ahead and appreciate fundamental changes that were in the making and that would make traditional modes of reacting to circumstances thoroughly counter-productive for them. Despite the next, nearly five-year interval of a Labour government, a severe and long-lasting reckoning was in the making. For the government, it meant the immediate rejection by the electorate, and even more important, a profound change not only in the leadership but in the broad orientation of the party.

59

The return of Labour to power was not a particularly joyous one for it in the circumstances of 1974. The legacy of the shambles of incomes policy and the exacerbation of relations with the unions led Labour to have exaggerated expectations of what it could achieve in these areas that the memories of its past experiences should have dispelled. The balance of payments had not turned significantly or lastingly favourable; and it continued to be troublesome. Indeed, the substantial inflation that preceded the coming into power of the new government had its inevitably unfavourable effect on the balance of payments, and by 1976 this was in full crisis, requiring urgent recourse to the IMF in circumstances of maximum unfavourable publicity for the government.

A stabilization programme was developed with the IMF which put the emphasis on fighting inflation by means which would, it was thought, also immediately restore the confidence of financial markets in the pound. The essence was to control the money supply and to cut expenditures. Significantly, and as an anticipation of later policy direction, the main emphasis in monetary policy was on controlling the money supply; and this demanded frequent changes in interest rates as well as another attempt by the Bank of England to restrain the total volume of credit by means of the so-called 'corset'. The consequent competition between government borrowing and the private sector, which became more attractive with the anticipation of higher interest rates, only aggravated the fiscal problem, i.e. that of financing the 'public sector borrowing requirement'. While other problems, including consequential troubles within the government and the party were far from absent, it was the financial aspect, internal and external, which was predominant. The government showed that it had undergone a measure of ideological conversion over the necessity for more stringent (or 'prudent') monetary and fiscal policies. In retrospect, however, these seem to have had the effect of not sufficiently pacifying foreign and domestic critics, while sowing dissension among the government's own followers. Too little and too late seems to be, once again, the way to sum up this phase.

For the sake of chronological convenience I have dealt with this period from the demise of the first series of post-war Labour government to that of the end of the second series in terms of alternation of the two main parties at the helm of our affairs. I do not, however, want this to be taken as particularly significant in relation to the economic performance of the country during this time. As I shall argue later, it would indeed be difficult to relate our economic fortunes, let alone the way in which we were ourselves responsible for them, to which party was running our affairs. The events of this phase in particular, largely because of the character of our problems, with their monotonous repetition of the balance of payments constraints, the intractable problem of preventing or even abating wage-push consequent upon inflationary pressures from other causes and the equally monotonous stop-go, do not throw a favourable light on any of the governments during this period. If one wished to grade performance only small discriminating good and bad marks could be distributed. The outstanding characteristic, if one abstracts from sporadic attempts at major reform (i.e. as distinguished from electioneering rhetoric), is a general faltering of resolve and a less than skilful tackling of problems as they arose. As I have repeatedly stressed, most of the time external circumstances were unpropitious or downright difficult and dangerous. But if, in Bridges's words (Robert, the poet, not Edward, the mandarin), 'conduct lies in masterful administration of the unforeseen', both parties come out deficient, especially as much that needed to be tackled could not really be described as 'unforeseen'.

A New Start? 1979–93

A critical analysis of this phase which brings us to the *terminus ad quem* of our story, is much more difficult than what has gone before. Even the account of the 1960s and 70s is about 'battles long ago' where a degree of objectivity can reasonably be expected and, I hope, has been achieved. For the last fourteen years one party, having an unprecedented series of four consecutive election victories to its credit, has held power continuously. There were important changes of personnel four years ago, but it is not yet certain whether there has been a change of direction. A search for policy errors can too easily appear partisan. This is especially so since the party came into office with the declared purpose of a 'new start', a claim it has not ceased to make even after this lapse of time. That claim was, moreover, defended with such vigour and supported by such intransigent appeals to eternal verities that opinions favourable and unfavourable to it were too readily identified with virtue and vice. Notwithstanding an initial appeal to the all-embracing, compassionate, doctrines of St Francis, subsequent attitudes had more the flavour of the medieval inquisition. Any attempt to treat this phase in much the same way as earlier ones requires a good deal of daring.

To understand the policies of this government under its first leader (for more than eleven years), and to a large extent since, we have to distinguish between three levels of analysis. There is the socio-philosophical foundation – or at least rhetoric; there is the next layer, an amalgam of economic principles, especially in their application to public policy; and finally there are the actual policy measures, including legislation, by which the first two elements were implemented (or meant to be implemented). I have not much to say here about the first of these, although I comment on it briefly in the next Part in connection with the question of the *agenda* of the state. I also refer there to the second element, particularly to the heavy reliance placed – or perceived to be placed – on the unencumbered operation of the market as the most efficient mechanism for allocating resources. Between these very broad generalizations based on Adam Smith, though involving a rather extreme exegesis of his writings, and the more day-to-day policies supposed to be derived from these basic principles, one can distinguish certain broad directions of economic policy. Of these probably heavy reliance on monetary policy figures most prominently. It has been regarded on the one hand as the most general and least specifically interventionist policy, and, on the other, as the most efficacious against inflation, identified at an early stage as the prime economic evil.

If more detailed directions of policy had to be distilled from these few simple points, they would probably run as follows. The 'frontiers of the state' had to be 'rolled back': too much of the gross domestic product is passing through the Exchequer, and by the same token 'government' ought to be 'taken off the back' of business. Free enterprise, i.e. the supply side will make for a better performing economy than can the state, which operates through a network of nationalized industries, detailed regulations, subsidization and demand management, which leads it to expansionist fiscal policy and lax monetary policy.

This set of arguments is not new, and much of it can be found in the *locus classicus*, Adam Smith's attack on the 'mercantile system'. There are a large number of more specific general propositions derived from them. The welfare state is an obvious target for attack, not only because it does offend against the principles of minimum government intervention, but also – and this has become even more pronounced in the more recent stages of government policy than it was at the beginning – because it is costly and therefore harmful to business on whom it is assumed the burden always falls. The trade unions are not only an unwelcome survival of earlier systems of intervention in the free market, but they also create an unnecessary burden on the entrepreneur and make business less competitive. 'Free' labour markets would avoid this. Attempts to involve the unions in broad policy making, which were a marked feature of earlier governments, including Conservative ones, are merely dangerous steps on the slippery slope that leads towards the corporate state.

To carry out policies based exclusively and rigorously on these principles in the teeth of the accumulation of practices and attitudes from the past, which always cling like barnacles to the whole parliamentary and administrative apparatus, would have been difficult for any government. Moreover, it is by no means certain that the man in the street, even if he marked his ballot

63

paper for the victorious party, would have welcomed an intransigent pursuit of all the policies in the party's manifesto.

Many inconsistencies in what was actually done throughout this period, often involving very considerable intervention by Ministers, together with a good deal of centralization of decision making despite an avowed intention to do the opposite, can easily be listed. Some of the departures from principle may well have avoided errors which strict adherence could have caused. However, the essence of the analysis must be an examination of the main strands of actual policy that were consistent with the government's intention and programme. A frequent complaint against economists is that, unlike the physical sciences, theirs does not afford the opportunity of testing theories in the laboratory. However, in this country and some others, notably in the United States, there have been many occasions when new governments have come to power determined to use the newly-given opportunity to try their theories in practice. From 1979 onwards, and for a great part of this last phase, this country was certainly exposed to a number of such experimental tests, though they tended to be of a more general kind than the specifics tried earlier, for example, in new taxation devices. What they all have in common is that they are not carried out in the laboratory, but on the *corpore vile*.

I do not propose to follow in detail the sometimes sinuous course of government on the many economic issues that confronted it, but to concentrate on three areas that are, in my view, the most important, and certainly the most characteristic. They are firstly the complex of macro-economic policy, particularly the emphasis on monetary policy in relation to inflation, growth and employment, and the exchange rate and international competitiveness in their international implications and repercussions for the balance of payments. Secondly, there is the government's policy in relation to developments in the European Community, which in one respect, that of the exchange rate régime, links very closely with the first group of issues. Thirdly, there is the question of industrial relations and the status of trade unions.

This, though certainly important, may not be considered by everybody as deserving a place among the most significant policy areas. It is, however, one which is widely regarded as having been a success for government policy. It has also been a subject of considerable political preoccupation from time to time. It is moreover certainly indicative of the general socio-economic thrust of policy.

Many other aspects, including one which, as I have said, has become more prominent recently, namely the future of the welfare state, belong to the same universe of thought.

As for the first complex of issues, it very quickly became clear at the beginning of the new administration that, not surprisingly when one looks at the preceding history, it chose the suppression of inflation as its principal target. This was more or less in line with its electoral commitment. It also quickly showed, particularly in its first budget, in July 1979, that, while cutting public expenditure was not to be neglected, the main use of fiscal policy was to ease the burden of personal taxation. This may seem a somewhat curious objective from an anti-inflationary policy point of view, but it was also an electoral commitment. For the rest, reliance on monetary policy, primarily through the instrument of short-term interest rates, was the main path towards the anti-inflationary objective, against a background of major innovations in financial markets, all of which had the effect of liberalization, and an increase in the availability of credit, which had already been initiated by an earlier Conservative government in 1971 through the policy of 'competition and credit control'.

The reduction in taxation, which benefited relatively more the higher taxpayer, added to the flow of funds into certain areas of consumption which showed a particular import propensity. As the effect of higher interest rates was *inter alia* to strengthen sterling, the combined effect was to favour imports and handicap exports. At one point the appreciation of sterling exceeded 40 per cent and led – to quote one example – Australian importers of British cars to complain that their market had completely disappeared. For some time, therefore, the net effect was unfavourable to growth and to the balance of payments, while the popularity of tax cuts as promised was diminished by being noticeably less advantageous at the lower income brackets.

It looked for a time as if the promised goal of reducing inflation could be achieved, whether concomitant unfavourable consequences were to be regarded as a tolerable price to pay or not. However, between 1983 and 1990, with only a dip in 1986, prices were again on an upward trend. Altogether the net change in the retail price index was insignificant during the first eleven years: from 10.3 per cent in 1979 to 9.7 per cent in 1990.

In the meantime, the heavy reliance on monetary policy had a bad effect on employment. However much one may agree that inflation is an economic evil, as well as a social and political one, if it is singled out as the only target for governmental action, and if one further regards it as an exclusively monetary phenomenon and therefore treats it exclusively by monetary means, and if monetary policy is handled primarily by interest rates, one is inevitably using a rough and ready instrument which hits rational and 'speculative' plans and projects alike. It therefore has a generally depressing effect on enterprise and employment. The idea that a restrictive monetary policy by itself can suppress inflationary expectations for any length of time without any effect on activity, growth and employment is not only not justified in economic analysis, but is not, as it turned out, supported by our own experience. Indeed, after the end of the first eleven years, and when the anti-inflationary consequences were at last beginning to appear, though without any early and significant improvement in employment, Ministers were beginning to admit that unemployment was a price that had to be paid for getting rid of inflation.

The history of the period shows quite as many ups and downs of economic activity as earlier ones, with equally fluctuating effect on the balance of payments, the exchange rate and the public finances. There certainly is no evidence that stop-go had been banished. This, the most puzzling of all the complex economic difficulties that have beset us, plagued this government as it has others. What is, however, questionable is the reliance – with extreme fervour and ideological zeal – on the monetary weapon as the main, if not the only, one to be used in the struggle to achieve sustainable, non-inflationary economic growth. It is this stubborn neglect of other policies, or their wrong or untimely application (as the extent and the precipitate character of the 1979 tax cuts) which is properly an object of criticism.

Although the broader socio-philosophical attitudes that were encouraged by government during this period are outside the purview of this analysis, it is relevant to mention that the spreading of a general urge for quick profits and high individual consumption levels against a background of credit expansion and general trade liberalization was not exactly conducive to the achievement of steady and balanced economic growth. The growth in the value of financial assets promoted by the fiscal and monetary policies worked in the same unfavourable direction. The explicit rejection of 'consensus' as a necessary or even worthwhile general condition for economic reform, the scathing references to the uselessness of the concept of a mixed economy or to that of 'society' were equally unhelpful.

The second area of policy I have highlighted is the government's attitude to Europe. As far as the phase here covered is concerned, it would certainly need detailed treatment to bring out the zig-zagging that marked the battles the government fought on the Community's budget and our contribution to it. Similarly, the contradictory attitude to the Single Act, with its significant strengthening of the decision making powers of the Community, the equivocal attitude to the resumption, after many years, of the Community's search for wider economic and monetary union and our refusal to join the European Monetary System in 1979 as fully co-operating members (something achieved in 1990) are examples of, at the very least, uncertainty and vacillation. For the purpose of this account what is significant beyond these specific aspects of our conduct is the general *leitmotiv* that ran through policy and rhetoric. Being the standard tune of the Prime Minister and a few other important Ministers

67

close to her, it was not surprisingly taken as the true expression of the British attitude, whatever compromises were made on particular points. 'Read my lips', particularly at the time of the Bruges speech, might well have been a correct instruction: it was in fact taken as such by most of our partners.

That all this was disadvantageous as far as our general relations with what were now our principal trading partners were concerned belongs to a different level of discourse. That it might have deprived us of some definite advantages is virtually unprovable except in one particular respect: the Exchange Rate Mechanism, the operational part of the European Monetary System. When we finally joined after it had been in existence for more than a decade, and almost certainly had been of benefit to its members, we did so, by all accounts, without adequate consultation with our partners on the rate. This was not merely a failure to observe the ordinary standards of conduct, but it must be remembered that by our entry our partners were automatically put under certain specific financial obligations. A very large body of opinion at home and abroad thought the rate was too high to be sustainable, given our general economic situation and particularly the balance of payments.

The situation, therefore, could not last, and indeed it came to an end in 1992 when we left the mechanism with an immediate substantial devaluation of sterling. The general monetary disturbance which followed, causing other devaluations and ending with a substantial increase in the margins of the mechanism, virtually suspended the Mechanism for the time being. It also made the originally planned move toward the third phase of economic and monetary union look unrealistic, even at the second possible date of 1999. The British government itself had decided to 'opt out' from joining it at all unless this was specifically voted by Parliament. To some this was of course 'a consummation devoutly to be wished'; and to them the whole episode was proof of the folly of our original entry into the Mechanism, and indeed of the whole process on which the Community was engaged. The whole episode showed an extraordinary vacillation in the government's attitude to the effect of major exchange rate changes: a rapid conversion from a 'macho' attitude delighting in a 'strong' sterling to the extolling of devaluation as a means of increasing our competitiveness.

The third area which is worth singling out in reviewing the course of the last fourteen years is the government's stance *vis-à-vis* the trade unions. As we have seen, this had been a fairly constant source of trouble for successive governments during most of the post-war period. Even Labour governments, perhaps more particularly Labour governments, closer in so many respects to the trade union movement and, therefore, supposedly better able to deal with it, had had considerable difficulties. It is undoubtedly true that towards the end of the 1970s the trade unions had achieved a substantial position of power, covering more than half the labour force with what was their highest membership – over 13 million. The series of disputes, the failed efforts at incomes policy and the bitter and debilitating strikes that had punctuated this rise in the numerical strength of the unions led to a significant change in popular attitudes. There was a growing general perception that unions were 'too powerful', and this gave rise, though less strongly and more slowly, to a feeling that the (new) government's plan to reform trade union law was right. The 'hubris' to which governments are so easily prone, particularly in the economic sphere, seems also to have infected the unions, at least according to general perception. They were therefore an obvious target for the government's reforming zeal; and this fitted in well with their other economic and social objectives.

I need not trace here in detail the disputes and strikes, notably the great battle of the miners' strike which so strengthened the government's resolve, the methods by which the government asserted its authority, the series of legislative reforms which it instituted and the resulting weakening of the unions. This is illustrated most strikingly by the decline in membership to $9\frac{1}{2}$ million by 1991, covering little more than one-third of the workforce. This particular aspect of the government's general policy is hailed by many as its one undoubted achievement. It certainly was effective, and as far as one can see now no early change is at all probable. Whether it has decisively changed industrial prospects is not certain. The question of wage bargaining, i.e. its structure and method, its relation to other macroeconomic questions, such as unemployment, growth, inflationary pressures and competitiveness (together with the related factor of non-wage social cost), is a most difficult area of economic analysis and policy and continues to be sharply debated.

One factor which may be mentioned here is that whatever may be the correct path through this thicket of problems, the nature of which incidentally varies a great deal from country to country, it is not yet clear that the threatened total disappearance of what the French so aptly call 'a valid interlocutor' would be wholly desirable. At any rate it could be argued with considerable justification that, in so far as wage-push inflationary tendencies have abated, the weakening of the trade unions was not the most important, independent cause. Unemployment, on the other hand, could be made responsible for the reduction in wage pressure and to a degree also for the weakening of the unions.

I said at the beginning of this account of the last phase of this chronicle that I would only deal with three aspects of government policy. This, however, is not to say that there are not a number of others that a fuller recital would need to include. Of all the ones I have left out, probably the one that would most readily spring to mind is the accelerated drive for deregulation and most of all the privatization of hitherto state-owned enterprises. I shall have something further to say about this in connection with the general issue of the agenda of the state. Deregulation is a catch-all term that is in general accepted by all political parties and by public opinion. That is not to say that its scope and its timing are not or should not be contentious. In fact, many specific actions in this area, which have inevitably involved new regulation to stop some of the 'side-effects' of deregulation are still much debated; and in some, such as the financial services area, one would have to be very bold indeed to claim that the current situation is not likely to be subject to considerable further change. I do not, however, think that any major specific errors of policy affecting our economic performance can be easily identified.

I take the same view of privatization in its more specific detailed sense. The urge to dismantle state ownership, sometimes preceded by the dismantling of state management, has been world-wide, affecting advanced industrial countries and others alike. The causes of this retreat from an earlier move the other way – not always associated with left-wing governments (see for example the nationalization of some French banks and industrial enterprises after the war) – are many and complex. About its course in this country in recent years, there may well be argument concerning details of the structures chosen, of valuation of assets and pricing of shares; and no doubt some things could have been done better. More weighty arguments would turn on the choice of sectors and individual enterprises to be 'privatized', particularly when it comes to public utilities and so-called natural monopolies. But reasonable people may reasonably hold different views from one another on these issues. That the government was largely ideologically motivated is no doubt true, but this does not by itself constitute an error of policy which can be shown to have harmed our economic performance.

PART TWO: Why

'This is a difficult country to move ... a very difficult
country indeed ...'

Benjamin Disraeli to Henry M. Hyndman,
quoted in Robert Blake, *Disraeli*

'Those Societies which cannot combine reverence to their
symbols with freedom of revision must ultimately decay
either from anarchy or from the slow atrophy of a life
stifled by useless shadows.'

Alfred North Whitehead

A Broader Explanation?

Can we leave the story where it has got to so far? Is there any need to look further into the ups and downs of our country in the last seven decades and the identifiable policies to which they can be linked? Are the recurrent themes of major concern – the balance of payments, unemployment, stagnation, Europe – sufficiently related to these specific policy actions to provide at least a coherent pattern if not an explanation? There are, indeed, some arguments for leaving the story at this stage. As I have repeatedly emphasized, many of the themes dealt with are common to the advanced industrial countries, even though their severity and the rhythm in which they appeared, has varied in each.

Moreover, it has to be recognized that British absolute economic performance in some areas has – though not consistently – been respectable. As for relative performance, there is comfort in the fact that what was the first workshop of the world could hardly be expected to maintain that position for a century and a half. Other countries have risen and declined, sometimes to rise again. In the end, could it not be that the fault is in our stars?

I share with many others the belief that this is not an acceptable view. The fact remains that our performance in recent decades has been poor, relatively, in two respects. Firstly, as compared to that of other countries of similar economic development, and sometimes poor even despite equal or worse devastation in two world wars, as in the case of Germany, Japan and the formerly occupied countries of the European continent. In the second place, our economic performance has been considerably below the level required to satisfy the many popular demands placed upon the economy.

Thus, to leave the story now would offend not only the most elementary instinct of enquiry, but also the unquenchable search for better performance in the future. This requires that the possibility of a more convincing explanation of the past should at least be attempted as an essential condition for future improvement.

This last point is the crucial one, for if it were at least possible to go some way further to explain past deficiencies, the chance of avoiding or remedying them in the future might be better.

If, notwithstanding the caution I urged earlier about the pitfalls in the search for a historical *causa causans*, some broader explanation of our uneven and so often unsatisfactory economic performance is desirable, how is it to be obtained? Also, how can one be sure that it is, if not wholly specific to Britain, at any rate particularly applicable to Britain in this particular time span? If we accept the list of errors of policy and their consequences on economic performance as a first statement of what has conditioned our economic destiny during the period reviewed, the question would then be whether there are features common to the way in which errors of judgement were made and the relevant policies flowing from them adopted. If such can be found, this would give a pointer to an explanation that would transcend the specific circumstances of each particular case. Is there something, for example, common to the return to the gold standard at the old parity in 1925 and the circumstances of our long-delayed entry and then sudden withdrawal from the Exchange Rate Mechanism of the European Monetary System?

Is there something in the way in which economic policy (within the political upheaval of the National government of 1931) was used to cope with the depression and unemployment that has a familiar ring when compared with the attitude of government to the prolonged recession of the early 1990s?

A 'Cultural' Theory?

There are various ways in which one can attempt to dig deeper in order to uncover a possible nexus between the discontents that have plagued us. One of these is to construct some broad hypothesis of the nature and cause of change and then to see whether the facts fit it as far as the economy is concerned. This usually amounts to constructing some broad 'cultural' explanation – in this case of one form or another of national decline. I use the word 'cultural' for this purpose to mean an amalgam of factors which cannot be totally subsumed under individual labels: economic, political or technological.

In a general sense such broad theories have forever been a well-known feature of historiography and of social theory. Examples abound both for individual countries, Greece, Italy, Holland, Portugal, and for the broad sweep of world history: Karl Marx and Oswald Spengler, for example. The 'decline of empires', the 'end of history' are more modern examples of earlier theories, such as 'the fall of the West' or the 'immiseration' of the working class and the prediction of the 'expropriation of the expropriators'.

Britain's history in the last century or two has not been spared similar broad-ranging theses. As these bear on the British economy to a considerable extent, they have a special relevance for the problem here posed. One thesis puts in the centre of its explanation the erosion, possibly the disappearance, of the spirit of industrial enterprise and has been much propagated in recent years. It runs in harness with the many fashionable theories of the decline of empires. This thesis specifically ascribes Britain's loss of her premier economic position to a process of 'gentrification' which has destroyed the eagerness for pecuniary rewards to be expected – and obtained – from the relentless pursuit of industrial ingenuity and application. The simultaneous single-minded search for greater material rewards and acceptance of the risks which this involves, which was, it is said, characteristic of early British capitalism, is no longer so. The values and practices of an earlier social structure have gradually asserted themselves over the new industrial classes and have weakened this earlier drive.

Masses of individual examples may be – and have been – cited in support of it, including pronouncements by eminent people, but they do not necessarily carry conviction. Many of them tend to identify the person's own view with some general national characteristic. 'We (the British people) do not like this,' or are 'attached to that'. These pronouncements are often so extreme as to recall the (perhaps apocryphal) petition of the three tailors of Tooley Street which began with, 'We, the people of England'! If there is evidence of a search for security by entrepreneurs, this is by no means a particularly recent development. One has also to observe not only that this is hardly a uniquely British phenomenon, but also that there are as many examples as ever to be found in Britain in recent decades of readiness to take risks and to satisfy an urge for money making that is as powerful as it was in the nineteenth century heyday of enterprise, or as it is in the 'tigers' of South-East Asia today. Moreover, if one wishes to seek out traces of a decline of the spirit of enterprise in the terms in which this is postulated for Britain, one can also readily find them in the economies which overtook the British some decades ago: the German, American and Japanese. In the latter case, in particular, the increasing difficulty of finding weekend accommodation in beauty spots, or the evidence of Japanese travellers amassing luxury goods in airport shops – to say nothing of the remarkable increase in foreign travel – shows that many Japanese have also discovered the truth of 'all work and no play . . .'

It is true that certain features of British society, such as the Monarchy and nobility, a still substantially hereditary (at any rate non-elected) second parliamentary chamber (though now containing a large number of those who have been successful in making money through business pursuits, including industry), the outward trappings of the operation of the legal system, the role of the ancient universities and many others carried through nineteenth-century capitalist industry by precept and example up to the present day, appear to show the persistence of pre-capitalist forms to which very many of today's representatives of industrial capitalism feel a need to conform. Be that as it may, it has had no significant effect on those representatives' continued pursuit of material success as measured in the terms of today's society. If the 'new' classes have been captivated by the manners of the old, it is no less the case that the old have only too readily succumbed to the realities of the new.

It is mistaken to take those survivals of what seems to have been a more leisurely and less money-devoted way of life (strawberries and cream at Wimbledon and Henley, or morning coats, top hats and extravagant millinery at Ascot as well as cricket on the village common) as significantly detracting from the reality of the trading rooms in the City or the new automobile plants in north-east England. They count for as much or as little as the obligatory dinner jackets at the Brenner Park Hotel in Baden-Baden or the splendid jewellery worn by the multitude of German ladies at the Salzburg festival. Examples can surely be found in the United States and Japan as well of the co-existence of the hallmarks of an industrial-pecuniary culture with either the survival of older or the grafting-on of new non-pecuniary values. The protagonists of the 'gentrification' theory might remember that it was an American economist, Thorsten Veblen, who wrote *The Theory of the Leisure Class*.

What I have said above in no way detracts from the fact that many rightly regard numerous aspects of present-day British society as being agreeably full of kindness and generosity, perhaps not so often found elsewhere. It may well be that those who are materially able to do so can construct for themselves in Britain a quality of life superior to that possible in other countries. But even if the resulting pattern derives some of its attraction from an older culture, this does not mean that the wealth creating activities necessarily suffer. Even more decisively it has to be stated that it would be extremely difficult to correlate the supposed process of gentrification either with the ups and downs of British economic performance or even with a secular tendency of economic decline in the last seven decades as here postulated and described. Even if a case can be made for the view that attitudes to different forms of money making have changed, and that manufacturing, particularly in the sense of William Blake's 'dark, satanic mills', or the American 'smoke-stack' industries, is less highly regarded than 'something in the City', it is, in any event, doubtful whether this is peculiarly British or, more important, that it is more marked now than it was at an earlier stage. If anything, it has been the other way round. Attitudes to different ways of amassing a fortune – and how to spend it when it has been made – always change and so does the social status of the protagonist. Nevertheless, there is no reason to think that many of those who do not know who Vespasian was have not fully accepted his doctrine of *non-olet*!

It is regrettable that this particular theory of Britain's industrial decline fails. It would have furnished not only an explanation of a whole series of complex phenomena, but also done so in a particularly attractive way. For it would have placed the ultimate cause of what at first appears as material worldly failure in the attachment to more seductive criteria of what constitutes a good society. Alas, this 'flattering unction' is not really available.

Manufacture *v.* Commerce and Finance

The explanation which rests on a theory of 'gentrification' has also been challenged by another cultural theory on the ground that it places too much emphasis on manufacturing as distinct from commercial and financial prowess, in which Britain has been, and, it is argued, continues to be pre-eminent. In extreme form, this view would necessarily lead to the conclusion that there has been no decline in economic performance. The proposition, which is common at one level of abstract economic theory, is that there is no difference in respect of wealth creating between physical production (manufacturing) – and, indeed, between the production of necessities and luxuries – on the one hand and services on the other. In other words commerce, which alters the time and location indices of goods, as well as finance, without which the link between production and distribution would be impossible, are as important as manufacturing and this underlies the critique of the gentrification theory. But in this form it cannot have relevance to declining economic performance, particularly if it is argued that commerce and finance headquartered essentially in London – unique in comparison with other industrialized countries in being overwhelmingly the centre of the most significant activities of British society – have always been predominant, and that the eminence accorded to manufacturing is both economically and historically a myth.

On the other hand, even if it is admitted that manufacturing (as a condition of, or at least an accompaniment to the activities of the commercial adventurers of the seventeenth century) was the foundation of Britain's economic prowess, it is argued that a shift has occurred in favour of trading and particularly finance in the hundred years between the mid-nineteenth to mid-twentieth centuries and that this may account for diminished economic performance. Traces of this view re-appear regularly in debates in recent years, when the role of the banks in Britain (including domestic versus overseas investment and the building up of an overseas empire as against domestic industry) is thought to be inadequate compared with countries like Germany and France, to which reference has already been made. These further reasons for rejecting the gentrification theory are substantial, even if their main positive aspects, namely to restore a balance in the view taken, particularly historically, of the respective roles of finance/commerce and manufacturing in accounting for the performance of the British economy are not easy to sustain.

Thus, neither view can contribute much to the explanation of what has been described and analyzed so far. Seductive as they are, particularly as they are often presented with considerable verbal brilliance and with a wealth of historical references, they leave far too many questions unanswered.

The trouble with all these broad explanations of the dynamism of historic change – from Marx's class struggle to Spengler's decline of the West – is not only the unsustainable reliance on one factor possibly important in itself, but also that they relate to far too long a time period: in the case of 'gentrification', for example, this is at least 130 years, while in the case of the one which denies that theory, the period is as much as 240 years. It is inherently highly improbable that the individual pieces of evidence cited in support of such theories can maintain their supposed validity over so prolonged a period. Certainly, they are useless for the purpose of analyzing the more recent two-thirds of this century here treated.

Economic Science and Public Policy

A more useful procedure is to separate out the different categories of ideas, institutions and practices from which the policies – good or bad – to deal with the major economic problems of this period sprang and to analyze their effectiveness. They broadly fall into two classes: firstly, the state of economics in its relation to public policy, and secondly, the machinery, political and administrative, through which the analysis and prescriptions of the science are applied in the practice of statecraft. Some reference will also need to be made to the international nexus. When this process has been gone through, it may be possible to revert to the question whether some broader link specifically relating to the character of British society can be detected. However, preceding the analysis of the economics of public policy, something must be said about the broader question of the reach that government action should have in the economy; what in the nineteenth century was called the 'Agenda' of the state.

The Agenda of the State

The relation between the state of development of the theory of economic policy and the nearly two-centuries'-old debate about the agenda of the state is a reciprocal one, though not necessarily one of direct linkage. In Adam Smith, the link is fairly direct: the analysis of the market and its *modus operandi* leads intellectually direct to a modest view of the proper scope for government intervention. Indeed, he begins his discussion of policy with a violent attack on the then existing remnants of mercantilist policies. More general is the argument against the state lending its legislative or administrative support to the creation or maintenance of monopolies. While it is very doubtful that Adam Smith was as completely wedded to a total non-interventionist view of state action as some present-day extremists claim, he must clearly be classed with the 'small government' view, which he derived not only from a basic social theory – as did so many other writers around that time – but from two other more specifically economic sources. These were the analysis of the role of the market mechanism in what we would today call the allocation of resources, and also the absence – inevitable at that time – of any discussion of what might be the economic instruments for what we would now call macro-economic management. The very idea of the existence of possible means of influencing economic performance by general measures rather than by direct intervention in specific markets had not seriously been thought of. The limits of state action were effectively summed up in the doctrine that it had to be much the same as the management of a family. Even Smith's celebrated canons of taxation barely touch upon the macro-economic possibilities of fiscal policy. He did, however, take a very decided view in favour of central control of monetary policy, a subject of secular if not millenary interest.

The situation changed in the next fifty years, by which time David Ricardo's analysis held the centre of the stage. His work, by implication at least, and despite the absence of any evidence whatever that he willed it, began to open up possibilities of greater government concern with the economy – without abandonment of the now-established theory of the market. Indeed, one of Ricardo's great explicit contributions was to extend the free market analysis of Adam Smith to the sphere of finance, including international finance and international trade.

Two principal reasons account for this apparently paradoxical change. Firstly, Ricardo had introduced a historical and dynamic social element into basic theory (which both Marx and his forerunners were not slow to exploit) by putting the emphasis on the distribution of the national product among the classes that have collaborated in its production. Secondly, his concern with monetary policy (a subject of acute contemporary debate, with the 'currency' and 'bullionist' controversy at its centre) directed attention to a potential macro-economic instrument, which had implications for inflation and the balance of payments that could be of great general consequence for the economy.

In the next 150 years the interventionist–non-interventionist debate continued, sometimes more vigorously, sometimes as just an underlying rumble to arguments about more specific economic policies. The popularity of each school has waxed and waned, perhaps not so much (certainly not only) with the standing of their broad social philosophies as with popular reactions to their specific effects on the economic position and welfare, whether real or only perceived as real. Of course, the development of more sophisticated analyses of how the economy works than Adam Smith's, and the simultaneous enlarging possibilities (whether for good or ill) of applying economic instruments to secure certain results, created new arguments for and against intervention, the latter being more in the nature of denials of fruitful results than of any results at all.

There are two broad areas of debate on the scope and quality of economic management that deserve examination: one, what the basic relation between the government and the economy should be; and two, the attention of government to short- as against long-term problems. What I am here concerned with is the role the state should play in economic management, as this question has, in theory and even more in practice, been answered at different stages in this history.

What can be said generally is that a reasonable balance between central direction and the absence of government involvement in the economic process has never been fully achieved. At times the asperity of the verbal battles over the correct principles to guide specific policies was greater than at others; and although for most of the period the pendulum never quite reached the extremes of its swing, there was enough uncertainty created to have an unfavourable effect on the factors that make for economic growth. The uncertainty was intensified by the fact that compromise was practised by both the major parties despite sometimes extreme ideological positions. Economic agents were therefore never entirely sure whether the political bark was worse than the bite; how far in fact the swings of the pendulum would go.

For a good part of the period ideological influences were on the whole kept within bounds as far as micro-economic measures were concerned, that is to say direct or indirect intervention that affected particular sectors of industry and trade, even though there were phases when sometimes one, sometimes the other tendency predominated. The last decade of the period under review is generally regarded as having marked a sharp break with the past in this respect and to have led to the abandonment of any attempt at the sort of consensus that had persisted for so long. But even here the pure doctrine of non-intervention was often honoured in the breach.

The six war years must be excepted. The first large modern war, involving more industrial power and attacks upon it and upon the morale of civilian populations than direct physical combat between massed troops, inevitably required complete control over economic activity from production to distribution. The allocation of resources, labour, capital, raw materials and finished consumption goods was soon brought under complete control and the fragmentary and rudimentary attempts of the First World War furnished useful lessons of what had to be done.

The period 1925 to 1939 (or very nearly to the year or so before the actual outbreak of war) is not easily classified in terms of the preponderance of a *laissez-faire* rather than an interventionist bias in government policy. Of course, the debate between the protagonists of the two schools never disappeared. Indeed, the increasing attention given to the Soviet Union (*Moscow Has a Plan* was the title of a popular book for the young) and the

85

apparent successes of a wholly command economy appeared very seductive to some. They compared favourably with the difficulties of the advanced countries and of the under-developed world with its burdensome commodity surpluses, notwithstanding continuing penury in their own and the richer countries during the turbulent 1930s. Thus professional economists and others increasingly turned to the study of 'planning'. That is to say they were increasingly interested in the possibilities offered by greater governmental intervention, ranging all the way from specific commodity stabilization schemes to a totally planned economic system in which reliance on private enterprise and on the market mechanism as the primary instrument for allocation and growth were virtually eliminated.

Looking back upon this period, it nevertheless seems to me that although it produced a vigorous and sometimes frantic theoretical debate, this was not strongly reproduced in arguments about specific issues; and the actual course of economic policy was comparatively little affected by it despite the interludes of the general strike, the short-lived Labour government of 1929, the crisis of 1931 and the ensuing depression. I do not mean to underrate the importance of the intellectual ferment of these years in political thought, public opinion generally and in economic theorizing. Nor do I want to suggest that the day-to-day political debate was not very acerbic. (See the vast literature on how to cure unemployment, what to do about monetary policy, particularly in the international sphere, or how to deal with a budgetary crisis.) What I mean is that despite differences of opinion the general question of the role of government did not as such appear prominently in the views of the contending parties. Perhaps as the only exception the future of the coal mines led to some general debate on nationalization. If Keynes's celebrated lecture, 'The End of Laissez-Faire', is regarded as evidence to the contrary of what I have said, it must be remembered that Keynes's broad plea for a pragmatically mixed economy with considerable emphasis on monetary policy – to come to full flower some years later – did not arouse the sort of virulent argument for and against among active politicians that has become familiar more recently.

It may be that my view is unduly influenced by the great part this debate has played in the political rhetoric of the last twenty years; or that the time span between the end of the depression and the outbreak of war was too short for it to develop fully; or again the fact that thought during these few years was so heavily concentrated on the rise and horrors of Nazism and Fascism as to push the question of *laissez-faire* versus intervention very much into the background. In any event, the war put an end to this debate; and when the possibility of dealing with these matters reappeared in 1945, the power of the ideas of the 1930s reasserted itself in a far more potent form.

Over many years the theoretical advantages of most state-run enterprises have proved to be illusory, and this experience has clearly been largely borne in on the parties of the 'left' everywhere, including in our country. How far the expected virtues of privatization will turn out to be realistic is not yet established in all cases. What is, I believe, clear is that this particular area of political argument should no longer be a major battleground. Much in the realm of supervision of these enterprises, their pricing policy and the application of monopoly and imperfect competition theory to many of them, will continue to be a fruitful field for analysis in applied economics as well as for political debate on practical measures.

What emerges from even a brief survey of the actual course of the argument over the agenda of the state is that it is not as central to the question of economic performance as that of macro-economic policy management (though that is, unfortunately, not nearly so easily cultivated a field). Perhaps one simple factor can show that extreme preoccupation with it is misplaced. Despite the political ups and downs and their consequences for economic structure, the proportion of GDP that goes through the public finances has not changed significantly over the years, despite governments' commitments one way or the other. Where 'agenda' arguments will clearly continue to be active is in the field of 'welfare', or, more neutrally, of transfer payments; that is to say, an area in which questions of strictly economic mechanism, for example a possible negative income tax or a continuous scale of tax and benefit, are very much interwoven with difficult social questions on which public opinion and its political expressions are not easy to determine or even to analyze.

Apart from its role in the intermittently extreme acerbity of British political debate, and its possible influence on economic performance, the fluctuating attention to the question of the role of the state in the economy has mainly served to add to the feeling of uncertainty inherent in the political cycle. It has, however, done so not as a broad philosophical question but rather in regard to the extent to which it predisposed governments to certain specific economic measures in the direction of greater or less intervention. As a rule it is not in the nature of the political process that the broad question as such should become an issue, but rather to provide a general rhetorical undertone to more mundane differences of opinion. This does not mean that 'sloganizing', at least against 'big' government, cannot be an important element at election time.

I will deal with this further below, but we must first consider in a more general way the influence of economics on the day-to-day activities of government during our time period. It can be said already that it is in regard to specific questions that the problem appears as a matter of practical politics: nationalization or privatization of a particular industry; should unemployment and sickness insurance be provided by the state or by private instruments?; the availability of state aid to particular industries; or the fixing of minimum standards of employment; in short, in regard to mainly micro-economic questions. Economics has much to say about many aspects of these problems: for example, the control and regulation of monopolies, especially of public utilities; the state's attitude to mergers; and the most efficient and reliable combination of measures to secure effective competition in financial markets while protecting the public from any misdeeds by expert operators. However, it is in the area of macro-economic

88

management, which affects the framework within which markets operate as distinct from the micro-economic intervention which changes the operation of particular markets, that the role of economics becomes particularly significant.

The Macro-Economic Instruments

There are two outstandingly important instruments for the conduct of macro-economic management: fiscal policy and monetary policy. Both of these have existed and been used in some form in all organized societies past and present of which we have knowledge; and particularly since the beginning of the nineteenth century both have played a major part in theoretical and practical debate. Even the most extreme advocates of 'small' government and non-intervention accept that in a modern society a substantial proportion of the national product has 'to pass through the fisc', i.e. as government revenue and expenditure; and they (or at least some of them) would also accept that the size and shape of the government's budget has an influence on the economy as a whole.

There are various degrees of opinion on the question of monetary policy. A very few extreme *laissez-faire* thinkers have gone so far as to favour the de-nationalization of money, while for practical purposes extreme monetarists would be content to see monetary policy managed by an 'automatic pilot' so as to produce as far as possible a 'neutralization' of money. And the majority of those of that way of thinking have specific views on how money and credit should be managed in specific circumstances so as to produce the same result, i.e. to avoid in general inflationary or deflationary impulses from the side of money affecting the real economy. Thus, leaving out the most extreme views, it is generally accepted that the state can influence economic performance, either directly, as in the case of fiscal policy, or through control over monetary policy. In the latter case, however, a strong body of opinion would extract the handling of monetary policy from the purview of the government and make the achievement of neutral money more likely by entrusting it to an independent authority, generally the central bank, with a specific mandate to ensure price stability.

Much of this debate has some relationship with attitudes to the agenda of the state, the fiscalists tending to the more interventionist, the monetarists to the more *laissez-faire* schools. For the first fifty-five years or more of our period this debate was generally confined to the theoretical arena, and it would, in my view, be difficult to identify the main political parties consistently with either one or the other school, fiscalist or monetarist. Nor can it be said that either of the main parties was always expansionist or restrictionist either in doctrine or in actual policy; their avowed attitude often following rather than preceding the course of the economy. Indeed, a reasonable case can be made for showing Conservative governments to have been more ready to indulge in spurts of expansionism than is generally supposed: Rab Butler's 'Invest in Success', the Maudling 'dash for growth', the 'Barber boom' and latterly the 'Lawson boom'. On the other hand, even without going back to Philip Snowden, there are examples of Labour governments expressing considerable anxiety, leading to highly 'prudent' and even restrictionist policies: Dalton's quoting Keynes: 'We are going down the drain at a great pace,' the 'Brown' paper of the first Wilson government and the July measures of the second, and Callaghan's 'We cannot spend our way out of a recession' are just a few samples.

This is not to say that, however difficult it may be to identify each of the main parties with one particular system of policy, there have not been major swings in the perception of markets and economic agents of what the parties claimed to stand for and what they would do when in power. While the swings of the political pendulum now and again produce more violent changes in the central direction of policy, even if these do not quite correspond to stylized patterns of party political philosophy, it is more on the popular perception, right or wrong, that electorates act. The years 1929, 1931, 1945, 1952, 1964 and 1979 might well have appeared at the time as marking colossal changes justifying the extravagant terms in which election slogans were couched. In retrospect, however, the alternation of political parties in government does not in general seem to point to it as the primary or most important determinant of economic development. There have been exceptions, and these must be carefully identified and analyzed. They were the occasions when a change of government has produced a qualitative change, which, even if it lasted only a limited time, left a residue which had a continuing influence. These exceptions seem significant, particularly the elections in 1945 and 1979.

It fell to the post-war Labour government elected in 1945 to implement policies which had been generated immediately before and during the war, and which were to have a revolutionary impact on society and the economy. The government implemented the Beveridge Report (issued 1 December), which, building on the Lloyd George social insurance reforms, aimed at creating what henceforth became known as the 'welfare state' – a comprehensive system of health and employment insurance and old-age pensions. It also committed itself to implementing the Employment Policy White Paper (May 1944), which, like similar legislation in the United States, acknowledged the state's responsibility for maintaining full employment. It also took the first steps towards 'economic planning' through the institution of an annual Economic Survey together with an elaborate expansion of the government's economic information gathering and publication service, including the forecasting of a wide series of economic data.

Against this background, the concern of government with the economy was greatly and avowedly increased, including a programme for the nationalization of a number of major industries and the Bank of England, representing 'the means of production, distribution and exchange', long a central item on the Labour Party's programme.

As already shown, these objectives had to be achieved in circumstances of world economic-political changes of exceptional magnitude presenting dilemmas of cruel intensity. In the international sphere, it also fell to this government to complete and adapt the results of the American Loan negotiations and the setting up of the Bretton Woods institution, the International Monetary Fund and the International Bank for Reconstruction and Development as well as the General Agreement on Tariffs, the substitute for an international trade organization, which had been intended to complete the international economic structure.

Undeniably, the framework within which the British economy operated was greatly affected by the general thrust of the policy of the 1945–51 government. It also contained important fiscal and monetary changes that were partly consequent upon the need to finance the new policies (e.g. transfer payments and nationalization) and partly founded on redistributive principles long cherished by the ruling party.

Without denying the magnitude of these changes, which were backed by popular opinion and in the broadest sense even enjoyed much support by other political parties, it must be observed that the circumstances, as always, prevented anything like a total adoption of the economic and social programme. In industry and finance, the immediate requirements of reconstruction and of the revival of the economy made recourse to entrepreneurial activities and talents necessary and moderated the centralizing, nationalizing tendencies. External factors, such as the conditions attached to the Lend-Lease settlement, the American Loan and the Marshall Plan, also generally demanded greater liberalization and the freeing of the forces of enterprise and the mechanism of markets. The constant external financial preoccupation with attempted and failed convertibility in 1947 and a large devaluation in 1949 were also major obstacles to full indulgence in more radical economic experiments.

Although government negotiators might continue to argue against the import of hothouse grapes or azaleas – 'toujours les azelées' complained a Belgian Minister about British arguments – not only the diplomatic but the economic pressures tended to soften the socializing zeal of the post-war Labour government. In any event, its life, as is usually the case, was too short to allow for more.

The ideological argument on the agenda of the state tended to subside; and by the time the political pendulum had swung back at the beginning of the 1950s, that front was not very active. The next and only other apparently major turning point came in 1979. I have already dealt with it in the brief account of the policy of the government that came to power in that year. Once again, one has to observe that, in practice, the pendulum did not swing as far back as the rhetoric of election manifestoes would have led one to expect. Nevertheless, the change in atmosphere and indeed in actual direction of government policy was marked. As in the previous phase of ostensibly fundamental change, it is by no means clear either how continuous and lasting these changes can be, or, more important, what precise effect they have had or will have on economic performance.

The Short-Term and the Long

No British government can count on having more than four or five years of power. Even if, as two Conservative-dominated series of administrations have done, they do in fact stay in office more than a decade, their long-term planning is inevitably somewhat constrained by the inexorability of elections, of which the timing is, however, unpredictable. This is not necessarily the only limiting factor. Throughout our period, perhaps most of all since 1945, the economic and, more urgently, the financial pressures have been insistent; and again and again governments have had to bow to them. Even if that has not removed their interest in longer term problems, these have not always managed to attract the careful study they require. Much of what falls under this heading has an important bearing on economic performance, even if they directly concern other parts of the socio-political spectrum. Many which thus tend to suffer from relative neglect fall outside my purview, although one of them, education and

93

training, even though it involves a wide range of other considerations, has undoubtedly a most important influence on the economy. Unfortunately it tends to enjoy fashionable interest only intermittently, as now in a period of high unemployment.

Important studies over a large field, including comparative ones that cover some of our partners in the Community, such as Germany, have shown a severe deficiency, both absolutely and relatively, to create not only an educated and cultured population, but, more specifically, a highly efficient and competitive workforce. Much is now being said both on the national and on the Community level about the need to improve educational standards and achievements, including the urgent one to reach an adequate level of training and re-training. This is considered essential if unemployment is to be cured – if only in part – by moving labour into new employments requiring new skills. It is also considered essential if Europe – and Britain – are to be able to face the competition of the newly industrialized and industrializing countries, particularly in Asia. This last point is often stressed in connection with the fashionable emphasis on the low relative unit wage and non-wage labour cost in these regions at a time when, it is argued, the acquisition by these same regions of most advanced modern technology is much easier than ever before. Theoretically, this particular aspect is debatable; but the case for more and better education stands in any event.

Much of the debate on education and training, particularly as far as Britain is concerned, turns on highly technical questions of institutional methods of both pre-job and on-the-job training and on methods of re-training and other means of making labour more mobile. These need not be considered here; however, what is clear is that the long neglect of these problems, and possibly also their being frequently combined with rarely fully understood questions relating to more general aspects of educational policy and institutions in this country, has had a disadvantageous effect on economic performance.

To remedy this sort of deficiency is one of the longest-term tasks that any society can set itself. No government during the whole of this period would have dared not to pay lip-service to the need to foster greater and more targeted training within and alongside a better general educational system. The means for doing so are, however, not only many and varied, but they do include dealing with deep-seated and often intractable traditional cultural aspects of society. This is not a subject which can be dealt with here, but it can at least be said that, if we are to judge by results, this has certainly been one of the major policy failures of successive governments. The frequent changes of the general educational framework have not been helpful; and it is at least reasonable to suspect that training as such has been too much conceived in terms of emergency programmes to be pursued in times of rising unemployment rather than as an integral part of the country's system of looking after what is its most valuable asset, its human capital.

More generally, the provision and maintenance of the country's infrastructure, including its physical and material one, and its continuous renewal to take account of major technical advances has often been criticized as inadequate. Failure in this regard is closely connected with fiscal policy, i.e. with the question of the provision of adequate funding for those projects in, say, transport and communication which need to be in part or even wholly the duty of the state. It is, on the other hand, connected with the more general question of the economic climate created by the character of the government's economic policy, as it bears on the willingness of the private sector to invest in long-term projects. The first part is contentious because it abuts on the problem of where to draw the limits of the agenda of the state; the second is equally so, because the precise effect of different types and mixtures of fiscal and monetary policy on the choices favoured by business are not entirely clear. They certainly vary from country to country and from time to time.

Successive governments have tried a variety of policies and specific measures in these areas, and these have always been highly debatable. The Labour government of the 1960s was particularly inclined towards direct and indirect investment incentives, perhaps beguiled by the facile analogy with the successes of what was our own agricultural support system before the preponderance of the Community's Common Agricultural Policy. This combined relatively free imports and the operation of the market mechanism to promote efficiency with a safety net for the individual farmer. The 'milk cheque' was something Ministers seemed to regard as only too easily applicable to industry.

Under later Conservative governments, continuing attempts to find similar devices when dealing with schemes that had to be state-funded came up against the constraints of a general tendency to tighten fiscal discipline. The emphasis on 'monetarism' and the reliance on interest rates in particular were a further constraint, for even in periods when short-term interest rates were eased, as would necessarily happen from time to time, this did not always stimulate investment, which is more sensitive to long-term rates. In any event, the course of inflation and that of interest rates was not always in phase so that real interest rates were often not attractive even when short-term nominal rates would have appeared so. Combined with exchange rate factors the changes in policy often had the effect of fostering foreign rather than home investment; and though this is not in itself disadvantageous in the broadest economic terms, it was often so because of its effect on domestic employment and because of its being in contradiction to the government's other economic objectives.

That much of our infrastructure is in need of renewal is undeniable, and successive governments must share the blame for this neglect. At the very least, there have been few if any examples of any systematic attempt to bring home to the electorate the character of this problem and of the choices available to deal with it. Nor has the necessary leadership to steer opinion in the right direction been applied. It is of little comfort to point to many other countries as showing deficiencies in this regards. The United States, which is also plagued with much derelict infrastructure, is so much larger an economy and has such a different tradition of mobility of enterprise, of physical capital and of labour that we should not assume that we can afford what it can.

One particular aspect of this general question of the long-term vista is that of the place of manufacturing industry within the economy. Until relatively recently, and leaving aside what empirical studies have shown, there was probably a general acceptance of the importance of having a flourishing manufacturing industry as the very basis of our economy. Labour and Conservative governments alike have, until the 1980s, shown no disposition to question a strong tradition, which is not surprising in the first modern industrialized country.

The strict economic analysis at a high level of abstraction going back to much of the late eighteenth/early nineteenth century economic teaching rejects the division of different economic activities on grounds other than their performance in the market. One great achievement of the classics was to sweep away traditional prejudices derived from medieval and mercantilist tradition of 'worthwhile' and 'not worthwhile' economic activity. Nevertheless, this abstract approach has never gained full reign in the assessment of different types of business within the actual circumstances of any given time and in any given country. Moreover, many preconceived ideas remained firmly fixed in the minds of the population at large as well as of politicians.

The secular tendency for a relative decline in manufacturing to the benefit of services, financial, commercial, and so on, here and elsewhere, was, however, too strong to be ignored. At one stage in the 1960s Labour governments, the observation that services were showing substantial relative growth even led the government to introduce the Special Employment Tax. This was based on the 'law' enunciated by a Dutch economist, Verdorn, that manufacturing industry was the principal engine of growth. The benefits did not come and this policy did not last long. At any rate, the tendency for industry to shrink certainly continued in this country from 1890 to 1989 from 44 per cent of total employment to 29 per cent.

In the mid-1980s, however, concern did begin to be fairly

widespread and a House of Lords Select Committee under Lord Aldington published a report in 1985 backed by much oral and written evidence from important industrial sources. This report, though inspired largely by the bearing of declining manufacturing on our export trade and its future prospects, examined all relevant aspects, including fiscal, monetary and other areas of macro-economic policy, and also furnished detailed international comparisons which delved into many other relevant considerations, such as education and training. In sum total, it was an extremely important report, covering both diagnosis and prescription.

After this lapse of time, it is not so important to consider what the report uncovered as the causes of relative decline of our manufacturing industry, or of the grave consequences which it thought followed from it, nor the direction in which it felt that remedial action was to be sought. What is most important and particularly revealing in relation to my major theme is the reception the report got from the government. Despite the inevitably restrained parliamentary language in which it was couched, the popular verdict that the government's reply was an attempt to 'rubbish' the report seems quite accurate. As such this reply is at once an example of the difficulty of getting governments to devote serious attention to admittedly difficult long-term problems and of the endemic tendency towards arrogance of power, which is certainly not conducive to the improvement of economic performance.

However, it remains the case that, despite the enormous number and variety of the economic issues that have crowded in on government in the last seventy years and that have been the subjects of an economic literature (both professional and lay) of almost unbelievable volume, the crucial general questions have increasingly tended to be reducible to issues of monetary and fiscal policy. Some governments, both left and right, have devoted a good deal of their energies to micro-economic problems; but leaving aside the issue of big versus little government – the former much more likely to be involved in micro-economic management – the major debates have always come back to tight versus lax monetary management and to more or less 'prudent' management of the national household.

How has economics served the policy makers in this ebb and flow of broad economic-political orientation? This is not, and cannot be, a history of the theory of economic policy; though I must note that, significantly, during our period, and particularly during the last forty years, a very large proportion of the new developments in economic science have not been concerned with economic policy, particularly with those aspects that bear directly on the problems of the day. The enormous development of analytical economics employing mathematical procedures, even when these have comprised the construction of models of the economy (of different degrees of abstraction from reality) upon which different hypothetical changes of policy are then made to impinge, have as yet been only of modest help to the politicians and their professional advisers, whether in or out of power.

A gap of increasing size has thus developed between perhaps a majority of academic economists and those of members of the public who try to understand the changes in the economy and, as voters, to decide which policies (and parties) to support. A casual glance at the learned journals and books reveals little. Economic analysts are increasingly being attached to governments – at the centre as well as in individual departments – but the difference in 'gearing' between academic research and the debates among and between senior administrators or Ministers is very great, the forecast often providing the only link. Indeed, it is over-whelmingly through the forecasting of economic change that the developments in economic analysis in the last half-century have been brought to bear on policy decisions. Forecasts based on models (which themselves contain abstracted relationships be-tween the main macro-economic categories: employment, budget-ary development, price movements, consumer expenditure [pri-vate and public], investment [private and public], interest and exchange rates, and so forth) are the major bases for policy decisions in so far as they are influenced by economics. For the rest, actual decisions are determined by party programmes, election pledges, tactical issues in current intra-party politics as well as between parties, and – again with considerable 'gearing' – basic social and political attitudes and the increasingly systematic study of ways of influencing public opinion, which is sometimes even termed a science. Even if the contribution made by economic analysis were more reliable than it has yet proved to be, one would have to be very bold indeed to give it the primacy over the other ingredients.

The Inadequacy of Economic Theory

It is not to condemn a great discipline – as economics undoubtedly is – to say that what it currently furnishes to the politician is not as useful as one would wish it to be or is sometimes thought to be by politicians and the general public. It is arguable that it is by its nature not capable of providing the sort of practical guidance physics renders to the engineer.

This sobering thought does not, however, quite correspond to the view of the relation between economics and politics held either by many politicians or by the general public, or, indeed, by many economists themselves. The spectacular growth in the use of economists in government (though examples of economics-trained top administrators are still quite few); the equally large increase in the output of economic and statistical information by government; and even sometimes the content of speeches in parliamentary debates and certainly budget statements (that would be quite incomprehensible to, say, William Gladstone) bear witness to the role which has now been assigned to economics in the process of opinion and policy formation.

Britain is by no means unique in this regard. In the first place much of the more recent developments in applied economics as they relate to public policy come from other countries, most of all from the United States; and that country is indeed in the forefront in the apparent use of economic – and particularly econometric – concepts in making, explaining and justifying economic policy. This appears also to be the case in many other highly industrialized countries, including Japan.

I say appears because, as in Britain, there is a large and not easily analyzed other mass of ingredients that go to the making of economic policy decisions. Even if one completely abstracts from these, it is not easy to correlate the use of economics in policy making with success or failure in economic performance. The difficulty arises in large part from the fact that basic concepts of economic policy – those relating to the crucial questions of monetary and fiscal policy – have been the subject of acute debate among practitioners of the science in the last fifty years or so, a debate that has also from time to time overwhelmed politicians. This debate, which is sometimes also related to the dispute between the big and the little government views, exists and has existed elsewhere; but certainly in the last twenty-five years it has been most acute and most characteristic of the British economic policy scene.

The Keynesian Revolution

The debate here and elsewhere is the direct result of the last great breakthrough in economic analysis since the long neo-classical, largely micro-economic-orientated, period from, say the last third of the nineteenth century to the 1930s of the present. This breakthrough was brought about by the evident failure of the policies based on existing traditions to deliver the economic results widely desired and expected. The greater part of that long period was marked by relatively simple economic precepts as applied to public policy: 'prudent' fiscal management (tight control of expenditure, moderate and moderately progressive taxation) and, as far as monetary policy and the international nexus were concerned, the gold standard with its classic 'rules of the game' managed by the Bank of England, i.e. tightening or loosening domestic money and credit in accordance with outflows or inflows of money. The search for new ways of thinking about economic policy was spurred by the increasing uncertainties after 1925, when a new pattern of international economic power emerged which precluded the dominant role of the Bank of England, the financial crisis of 1929–31 and the subsequent world-wide depression, and led to the revolution in the mid-1930s that is forever associated with the name of Keynes.

In Britain, its native place, it quickly won substantial support both within the profession and among substantial numbers of political practitioners. Within a few years the reaction against the orthodoxies that led to the policies of the National government of 1931, based as far as macro-economic management was concerned on the 'candle-end' principles of the May Report, had been widespread and profound. It was no doubt strengthened as far as popular acceptance went by dissatisfaction with many unpopular policies of the period in quite other areas, for example appeasement of the continental dictators.

The revolution was not confined to Britain, although on the Continent, with the exception of the Scandinavian countries, it was more subdued. It had, however, an even more triumphant progress in the United States, where Keynesian ideas, often refined and further elaborated, soon swept through academia and, with the Rooseveltian 'New Deal' and after, became a pillar of economic policy wisdom against which, at least up to the outbreak of war, the old orthodoxy was relatively powerless.

The purely intellectual debate over the new ideas was stilled during the war. Nevertheless some war-time economic policies were influenced by them, supplemented and supported as these had been with advances in statistical techniques relating to national accounting. In the immediate post-war period the problems of reconstruction and recovery and the adaptation of financial and commercial relations to the aftermath of war gave further opportunities for Keynesian ideas largely centred on 'demand management' through fiscal policies to be applied, though now again under challenge from revived more traditional neo-classical doctrines.

It must be noted that both the academic and the political

debates in that phase, i.e. during the first few years of the 1945 Labour government, were not exclusively concerned with Keynes-inspired fiscal and monetary policies, though these played a very important part. There was much else in that 'planning' and 'nationalizing' period (as already referred to) that went hand-in-hand with these policies. The whole intellectual complex of micro-economic intervention through the continued (war-time-inspired) 'sponsoring' Ministries, of nationalization (attempted or actually carried out) and the general concepts of periodic economic surveys with their forecasts led to broader attempts to revive and strengthen the pre-war interest in planning. These can now be clearly identified as having given a characteristic appearance to British economic policy making. From the point of view of the analysis I am attempting here, it was not only a more complete break with the past but in a sense a more extreme and doctrinaire era than Britain had known for a long time.

There was relatively little that was new in the age-old Labour commitment to national 'ownership of the means of production, distribution and exchange', or even in the greater emphasis on the planning concept. What was new was the incorporation of new economic ideas – in their most simplified forms 'deficit financing' and 'cheap money' – as means to foster growth and employment. These concepts were not confined to the Labour Party but were also influential in liberal circles and in the more moderate sections of conservatism. However, as it turned out, it was precisely these new ideas that proved to be more long-lived and more significant in moulding the policies of the left and of progressive opinion generally in subsequent decades.

Despite the defeat of Labour in 1951 and the subsequent, unprecedented twelve years of Conservative government, there was no clearly visible early counter-revolution in regard to fiscal and monetary policy in practical terms, although, particularly towards the end of the period, the so-called monetarist anti-Keynesian counter-revolution was increasingly powerful in (or around) academia, while Labour's other policies in the industrial field were halted and reversed.

Political Parties

We must now examine the relation between the economy and the arena of politics, in which ideas and the positions of power which enable these ideas to be applied in practice challenge each other. In our society, the main guardians of political ideas are, or claim to be, political parties, particularly at election time. I have already given examples to show that a general identification of the two main political parties with one or other macro-economic policy doctrine may be unsustainable. Nevertheless, popular perception, particularly in the short term, does tend to make such an identification. It may therefore be useful for a start to look at the 'electoral cycle' and to test it in relation to the succession of trends in economic ideas and policies, especially as the 'electoral cycle' has often been blamed in recent years for sharp policy changes. While it is clearly responsible for some ups and downs of economic policy, and (with due allowance for other factors) for some differences in economic performance, it is doubtful whether it can always be said to bear a major responsibility. During a considerable part of the period reviewed, the changes brought about by changes of government (as distinct from expectations created by election manifestos) were not radical.

It is, of course, a well-known fact, here as in many other countries where the electoral system and the mechanics of election permit it, that governments try to engineer a boom before an election. This is, however, not always in their power; nor is their subsequent performance, if they are elected, always in conformity with their preceding actions or promises. More broadly speaking, however, even though a real cyclical relationship as such is difficult to establish, one cannot dismiss the effects on the economy of the ebb and flow of party government as perceived by every individual or institution in their daily economic activities. It is arguable that, for example, during the nearly fifty years since the end of the war, the consciousness of the inevitable periodic electoral battle that could provide a radical change of policy has had a dampening effect on the economy. There are many indications that lead to the conclusion that the uncertainty created by the electoral cycle not only affected directly the public sector, but has also unfavourably affected economic decisions in the private sector in the short run. It has, therefore, had a generally weakening effect on the factors that promote economic growth in the longer term.

It is not possible to prove beyond doubt that a climate of relative tranquillity, due to a less acerbic economic-political debate is more conducive to economic advance. It may not, however, be fortuitous that a generally better relative economic performance appears to have been achieved in periods containing more of a basic consensus, even if they could not be altogether devoid of political agitation.

However, even if a more precise relation between the political ebb and flow and economic performance could be established than anyone has yet managed to do, it is difficult to see what clear conclusion could be drawn. Apart from argument about such specific matters as fixed *versus* variable terms of government or the 'first past the post' system of election *versus* some form of proportional representation, no serious person who has reflected on these matters has suggested that the broad political framework can be anything other than one which is subject to periodic review, renewal or revision by the 'grand inquest' of an election between organized political parties.

'Great Britain Ltd'

It is true that suggestions are heard from time to time that this or that aspect of economic policy (or possibly its whole broad orientation) should be 'taken out of party politics', as is sometimes also suggested – and now and again even achieved – in certain areas of foreign policy. The difficulty about these ideas is two-fold. First and foremost, while some economic and political philosophers may argue that fundamental interests could be served by the right policies regardless of which party may be responsible for them, this is not the everyday perception of the average citizen. In a developed and civilized community such as ours the sort of talk heard in recent years that there is 'no such thing as society' or that consensus is undesirable is patently absurd, and even damaging. It is nevertheless true that on many specific economic matters, from trade union legislation to social security, opinions differ, often sharply; and these differences will find their expression through the machinery of party politics.

It could be argued that there are other matters less directly impinging on the economic interests of different groups which could be made to form a common ground of desirable economic policies, for example, the status and function of the Bank of England. These could be taken out of party politics or, at least, the vehemence with which they are debated could be diminished. This area would presumably contain much of what is called macro-economic policy or economic management, including many of the propositions and instruments discussed earlier.

Is this a more realistic hope? The recent innovation which has associated a number of outside economists with the forecasting work of the Treasury (which is so central to its advisory role on economic policy to Chancellor and Cabinet) shows some inclination on the part of the authorities to think that the answer is 'yes'. One difficulty is that even if the answers of different economic experts to these problems were more or less the same (in the case of these new outside forecasters this is rarely likely), these answers would concern situations that are still very abstract compared with those which confront policy makers. These are specific and peculiar within a certain time frame. The path is long and torturous from the textbook or learned article, or even more general forecast, to a situation that requires a govern-mental decision on, say, interest rates, foreign exchange policy or the broad thrust of fiscal policy at a particular moment of time. There is, in short, considerable 'gearing'; and by the time the moment of decision is reached whatever scholarly consensus may have existed at the general, abstract level will probably have disappeared. Nor, unfortunately, is there a body of economic theory, let alone a theory of economic policy, that is subscribed to by all 'experts', even at the most abstract level.

Moreover, the methods by which economic political debate is carried on are now probably more aggressive than hitherto in modern times; and even if examples of vehemently contentious political argument can be found during the last century, the contestants were partly economists and partly the active politicians themselves. The participation of the 'great public' did not extend far; and while it may have had views on, say, free trade *versus* protection, it hardly participated in the battle of pamphlets that occurred; and the sophisticated arguments of the 'currency school' *versus* the 'bullionist school' would have left it indifferent.

Today, a far wider section of the population has some knowledge of the elements of the economic debate; and modern methods of communication ensure that the debate – even if its quality is misleadingly simplified in relation to often very complex matters – is widespread and continuous and carried on in terms which make it incumbent on even the most mild-natured politician to be highly combative. It is easy to see that any inherent tendency of the political pendulum to swing will be aggravated where the problems are difficult and often lack a consensus of opinions among the experts, and thus lead either to a more marked differentiation between the attitudes of political parties, or at any rate, to the appearance of it: all to the further bewilderment of the average citizen, not only in his political attitude, but in his own economic activity.

The Politicization of Economic Opinion

Is Britain particularly exposed to this phenomenon compared to other countries of a similar level of development? This is an extremely difficult comparison to make without ranging far and wide into, for example, the two-party system in the United States (and virtually in Britain), the multiplicity of parties in France and Italy, encouraged as many say by the electoral system, the mixed system in Germany and, perhaps even more so, the role of television, radio and the press in each country. What does however seem to be clear is that the factors enumerated earlier seem to have become both more variable and more potent. Combined with a recent tendency for the publicity surrounding the Prime Minister to grow, and for his traditional position of *primus inter pares* to change into a quasi-presidential one, this has led to a considerable politicization of economic opinion, which has spread to the threshold of the ivory tower and sometimes even into it with the greater use of outside experts as ministerial, particularly prime-ministerial, advisers as distinct from the regular civil service machine. The same tendency can be observed elsewhere, particularly in the United States; but to me at least it seems most marked in Britain.

The character of the machinery by which policy decisions are made and executed is more difficult to assess as far as its influence on policy is concerned, as also is the manner in which economic analysis is brought to bear on policy decisions, particularly in the economic sphere. The first resolves itself largely into the question of the governmental machine; not so much as far as its constitutional elements are concerned or in its correspondence to different political theories, as in the practical way in which specific decisions are reached, particularly those which hindsight has shown to have had a seminal influence; and, in this context, the role played by permanent and temporary advisers to the elected members of government.

The second opens up the exceptionally difficult question of whether economics has advanced sufficiently towards an adequate level of understanding of the economic process and a better set of prescriptions for influencing it. Here the analogy is often made with medicine, i.e. what progress has been made in clinical observation, diagnosis, prescription and treatment? Indeed, the medical analogy has played a particularly prominent part in the rhetoric used by British politicians. Their speeches and the writings of commentators and 'opinion formers' have been peppered with phrases suggesting malignancies, symptoms of ageing, false diets, and so on. This part of the economy has been starved; that has been allowed to grow too fat. Cures range from cold baths to a strict diet producing a 'leaner', fitter economy or the riding of bicycles to cure unemployment. And even Dr Emile Coué, with his famous cure of reciting, 'Every day in every way I am feeling better and better,' has been imitated (without acknowledgement).

Whether this type of political phraseology has been productive of more public enlightenment rather than of the creation of more prejudice is debatable.

This is not the place to go into the details of the structure of the British Civil Service and changes in it, from the Northcote-Trevelyan reforms of the last century to the latest experiments with executive agencies, or the contracting out of various tasks to private enterprises. The relevant questions are, firstly, whether the relation between the policies of successive governments, either as claimed by them particularly during elections or as actually practised when in power, and the 'machine' – particularly at the highest administrative level – can be shown to have some identifiable and significant bearing on the performance of the economy. The second question, which is more difficult to answer, and is not suitable for detailed treatment here, is whether differences in this relationship between Britain and some other highly advanced countries can be said to have a role in creating differences of economic performance to any degree.

The Outside Advisers

One aspect of this problem obtrudes very quickly: the role of 'outside' advisers, i.e. not regular members of the Civil Service, in helping Ministers to arrive at policy decisions and, to some degree at least, in carrying them out. At first glance, this role seems to have increased in recent years when measured both by the numbers involved and by their influence.

One cannot be sure that this first impression is correct without very painstaking and perhaps in the end fruitless research. One has to guard against one optical illusion. Although the regular Civil Service is no longer as shielded from publicity as it once was (this applied particularly to the Home Civil Service as distinct from the highest ranks of either the diplomatic or the fighting services, who always enjoyed some degree of freedom), it is still very much the exception rather than the rule for civil servants to be much in the public eye. Some outside advisers at least have been under less constraint in this regard; and since they are, almost by definition, closer in their political views to the Ministers they serve, they appear more frequently in the public prints and media generally, thus giving the impression of a larger and more influential group than they perhaps are. Nevertheless, it seems to be the case that the number and influence of outside advisers on Ministers has been steadily increasing in the period here reviewed, and particularly since the end of the Second World War.

I say that one cannot be sure because there have always been 'grey eminences', individuals with no formal position in the machinery of government, or only an *ad hoc* one created specifically for them, and some of these have exercised considerable influence on their political friends: Lloyd George and Ramsay Macdonald come readily to mind. Nor is this entirely unknown in other countries: Woodrow Wilson had his Colonel House and Roosevelt his Harry Hopkins. Sometimes, a regular public official achieves a particularly close relation with a powerful statesman, though in Britain this happens more rarely. Lord Normanbrook was probably as close to Harold Macmillan as an eminent civil servant could get, but his position as Cabinet Secretary and Head of the Civil Service served both to sanction the degree of closeness and yet to preserve a certain distance.

However, the tendency for Ministers and Prime Ministers to resort more to, and rely more on, the advice of people outside the

Civil Service has been, I believe, a special feature of the last three or four decades. Among the possible explanations, three come to mind. Firstly, the great expansion of the areas with which government is now concerned, and the complexity of the problems likely to arise within each, has made it less obvious that those in the higher reaches of the administrative service, who are still to a large extent 'generalists', if not quite as much with an exclusively classical education as they once were, can provide the technical advice often required without help. The service itself has responded to this development by creating new, specialist branches and offices and widening the sources of recruitment.

The second explanation – in part an aspect of the first – is the experience of the war with its very great influx of temporary civil servants, partly, but only partly, to cope with the general increase of the administrative machinery, but more in response to specific, technical war-time needs, of which the application of certain aspects of economics and statistics was an important one. Despite the inevitable pressure after the war, not only to cut down numbers, but more generally to return to former practices and attitudes of mind (already noted), a substantial part of the new personnel and, more important, of novel ways and procedures remained; and with these, a greater readiness to resort to the temporary help of outside advisers.

Advisers and Courtiers

Most important and intriguing of all is the evidently greater desire on the part of politicians to supplement and widen (and often to supersede) the normal, official channels of advice and seek help from individuals outside the hierarchy, not so much because of their greater specialist knowledge, as of their political, and often personal, closeness to the politician concerned. For this phenomenon, there is no close analogy elsewhere. In the United States, the top administrative posts below Cabinet Ministers, who are themselves technical advisers and delegates of the Chief

Executive, the President, are in any event to a very large degree political and change with the change of President. In France the existence of the *grandes écoles*, of the elite corps, like the *Inspection des Finances*, *Ponts et Chaussés* and *Mines*, the *Court des Comptes* and the *Conseil d'Etat*, together with the top school for administrators, the *ENA*, has created a situation in which there is a considerable flow from political to high administrative appointments with also a flow between them and the highest business appointments (partly because of the substantial number of state-owned enterprises). Certainly, as far as British civil servants are concerned it is only relatively recently that there has been any flow between the service and business. That between the service and politics has always been negligible.

In Britain at least two post-war occasions have provided particular evidence for the phenomenon of the outside adviser: 1964, when a Labour government succeeded after twelve years of Tory rule; and 1979, when a Tory government under a Prime Minister particularly anxious to be seen to be radically innovative came to power after a period in which there had been a number of Labour governments. (A somewhat similar situation arose in Canada, which, in terms of Ministerial/Civil Service relations, has perhaps the closest resemblance to our own, when the conservative Diefenbaker government followed a long period of liberal governments.) On both occasions there was clearly a suspicion on the part of incoming Ministers of the body of advisers who had for so long served 'the other side', particularly so in Britain in 1979. This did not, however, lead to any extensive or exceptional movement of personnel, but rather to the infiltration into the machine of personal confidants of Ministers; 'whisperers', as one of them once described his role to me.

Sometimes, such advisers are grouped into special units forming a kind of auxiliary mechanism to regular departments; and members of regular departments are sometimes seconded to these units, which may help establish working relationships with the departments themselves. There are a number of examples of these organizational devices during the period I have reviewed, but since most of them are based on the personal views and idiosyncrasies of Ministers they cannot be examined systematically. However, two aspects deserve some mention. One is the occasional major reshuffling of departments of state or subordinate Ministries due to supposed major changes of the directions and priorities of government policy (or, at least, revealing or concealing these). The other is the tendency for the politically compatible outside adviser gradually to become more and more like a courtier. When this tendency accompanies (as it very naturally would) the emergence of a more 'presidential' Prime Minister, the scene could well be set for a more radical transformation of the machinery of government than is perhaps intended, or, at least, clearly observable at the time.

Tensions between Ministers are bound to grow when collective cabinet responsibility clashes with 'presidential' direction; between departments of state (always possible owing to the varying influence of the Ministers concerned, but made more likely when the 'pecking order' of Ministers is more strongly determined by their relation with a more powerful Prime Minister); and between the regular public servant and the intimate outside adviser. The modern British Civil Service has managed to preserve for a century and a half an enviable record of impartiality – indeed often showing examples of fearlessness – in tendering advice to different political masters. The number of cases in which preferment seems due to political partiality, of which one sometimes hears, are minimal and usually unproven. This situation is to some extent helped by the very existence of the outside adviser, whose political closeness to the Minister is usually patent. Nevertheless, the development of a courtier-like attitude, and even of a courtier class, cannot be ruled out; and when it occurs, it is bound to create tensions and increasing strain on the official adviser.

It is quite impossible to demonstrate how far this development has actually taken place during our period, and, if so, what effect it has had on policy formation and execution and, in the end, on economic performance. It is in the nature of matters of this kind that they should remain hidden with only the very occasional emergence into the light of day, and then only as vague rumours. The underlying developments, however, are sufficiently clear: the intense politicization of economic opinion, the increasing acerbity of public debate on economic issues, the greater vehemence of the electoral battle and the new status of the Prime Minister (which the role of the media has fostered and makes almost irreversible). These, especially the last, make the above-mentioned consequences for the machinery of advice virtually inevitable. Perhaps this trend will not only continue, but may become – no doubt over a considerable time – so powerful that we shall see a situation not unlike the American one, where the highest departmental posts, now in our country clearly Civil Service ones, become virtually political, changing almost completely with each change of administration. The separation of the middle and lower executive activities of government service, which are in train and are often in any event the consequence of privatization of hitherto state-owned and managed enterprises, would facilitate such a process.

The Structure of Departments of State

Another aspect of the question of how the machinery of government relates to policy is that of the organization and functioning of departments themselves. Both in the First and the Second World War new departments had to be created to respond to new areas of government activity called forth by the needs of war. By the same token the end of war has brought forth new needs which have altered the scope of existing departments and created new ones. These changes are often accompanied by considerable debate both within government and in public, if only because they result in important changes in the power and status of individual Ministers' power and status. The disappearance of the Ministry of Food some years after the war and its absorption into the Ministry of Agriculture (Fisheries and Food) was an obvious example of the lapse of the need for a 'sponsoring' department for the food industry, but also of the fact that, in an unregulated market of more abundant food supplies, the consumer was considered identical with the mass of citizens, while agriculture continued to represent a defined producer interest. Generally these changes are not of fundamental importance. Even when they appear to be so, such as the creation of mega-departments, presided over by a Secretary of State and subdivided into Ministries, the net effect on policy making is rarely highly significant unless it is due to or accompanied by the rise of a powerful Minister, who may then exercise a special influence for a limited time.

The more general structure of the government has been debated from time to time and various plans propagated, including proposals for strengthening the collective decision making process of the Cabinet by, for example, enlarging the Cabinet Office and creating a staff designed to serve the Prime Minister and his colleagues in two ways. On the one hand they would examine and resolve long-term issues, which tend to be neglected owing to the pressure of day-to-day business, and on the other they would help in the ordering of priorities of the latter which would otherwise be determined by the relative competitive strengths of individual ministers. But as I have said, these suggestions, even when implemented, which to some extent they already have, have rarely made a great or lasting difference to the operation of the machine, certainly not nearly as great as the varying personalities of Prime Ministers or the changing personalities and effectiveness of special advisers.

In recent years only one major reorganization of the government machine has consciously and with great publicity been based on the avowed need for better economic performance, namely the creation of the Department of Economic Affairs in the first Wilson administration under a First Secretary of State, the acknowledged 'number two' in the government. This is not the place to go in detail into this experiment, which was short-lived in the end. (I have done so elsewhere.*) It is, however, necessary to mention it here because it was ostensibly the result of a certain diagnosis of the causes of our relatively poor economic performance after twelve years of government by one party.

Briefly, the theory was that the overwhelming power of the Treasury had resulted in too narrow a constraint over economic growth. Its concern – exclusively it was argued – with financial matters, i.e. essentially fiscal and monetary policy, had resulted in the neglect of both long- as against short-term interests and, virtually concurrently, the financial as against the 'real' economy. Whatever mistakes could be detected in the management of the economy during the previous twelve years could, it was thought, ultimately be put at the door of the Treasury, the all-powerful department, but one hampered by its lack of knowledge of the 'real', particularly the industrial, world and by its traditional devotion to the saving of candle-ends as the ultimate wisdom of statecraft.

We can leave aside the obvious exaggeration, amounting almost to travesty of the then existing function and outlook of the Treasury. We can also acknowledge that the distinction made between the 'financial' and the 'real' economy – one which curiously was to reappear briefly in a subsequent Conservative administration – was far too facile and contained half-digested elements of earlier debates on planning, and particularly a new emphasis on the French system of 'indicative' planning. This seemed to have scored major successes in post-war reconstruction in France, particularly in the creation of successful investment, not only in the revival of old, but also the creation of new industries. There was also possibly lurking behind these organizational ideas some element of the Keynesian *versus* anti-Keynesian controversy on fiscal and monetary policy which had briefly appeared in the first post-war Labour government and was to come to full flower some years later.

Whether the experiment failed because of a flaw in the concept, the unresolved personal differences between the three principal

* See Eric Roll, *Crowded Hours* (Faber and Faber, 1985; reissued 1995)

members of government, the overwhelming importance of the balance of payments problem (highlighted by the volatility of sterling which necessarily gave the Treasury – with the Bank of England – the star role in day-to-day activity) or because the power of the Treasury (of which the Prime Minister is First Lord) could not be expected to yield to a somewhat clumsily launched attack is not really important. Quite apart from these considerations it could well be argued that the mixture of old-fashioned planning ideas, i.e. virtually as part of a command economy with more modern notions of micro-economic measures (regional policy, subsidies, investment incentives and other discriminatory tax devices) to stimulate the private sector and the setting of planning targets in a disparate bundle of policies in which nationalization on the one hand and governmental 'spotting of winners' in the private economy on the other jostled each other was highly unlikely to be effective. And it is seen as particularly unlikely when it is remembered that the government had at first an exiguous, later somewhat larger, majority, and when it was faced with a thoroughly hostile financial climate which made respect for domestic as well as foreign financial requirements of overriding importance.

Incomes Policy and the Role of Trade Unions

One experiment that went down with the disappearance of this new department is worth mention, namely the renewed attempt to find an incomes policy, firstly on a voluntary, then on a statutory, basis that could, it was thought, make a decisive contribution to securing sustainable non-inflationary economic growth by restraining the spirals of wage increases and inflationary expectations which had so often plagued the economy.

I have already dealt with the basic aspects of this problem as one of the continuing themes of the British struggle for a pattern of economic policy that would lead to more successful economic performance. As I have shown, this issue is closely connected with that of the role of trade unions in the process of economic policy formation and execution and the attitude of government to it, which has varied considerably during our period. Incomes policy reached a high point in the short-lived Department of Economic Affairs, when it became virtually the only one of its activities with any significant impact on economic debate and on economic reality. Although attempts to evolve an incomes policy, with the corollary of a co-operative attitude by and towards trade unions, had been made before, and by Conservative governments, the more energetic efforts to this end in the early and mid-1960s led to a conceptual backlash. This took the form of the charge that a rapid move towards a 'corporate state' was happening, an argument which furnished an important element in the subsequent evolution of the opposite political tendency, in which it married happily with emphasis on the 'free market' anti-Keynesian, largely monetarist macro-economic policy within an overall 'philosophy' of 'small' government and 'rolling back the frontiers of the state'.

Although the charge of a rapid progress towards a 'corporate state' during the period of labour governments in the 1960s and 70s was grossly exaggerated, it was nevertheless true that the intensity of the relationship with the trade unions was greatly increased. The greater emphasis on the 'tripartite' National Economic Development Council (though this had been created by an earlier government), the negotiations over incomes policy and the beer and sandwiches evenings at No. 10 all created the appearances of something more than the reality of economic relations could actually sustain. It contained at least as many dangers to the better functioning of the economy as it held out hopes of removing some of the road blocks to growth, such as wage-induced inflation.

It became part of the hubris of the governments of the time, who thought they had a more powerful lever on the economy and on relations with trade unions (in which many of the Ministers had their roots) than was justified by the extent or depth of the political support which they could command. More important, as far as the role of the trade unions in economic policy making was concerned, were the changes, as yet barely perceptible but soon to become obvious, in the traditional British trade union structure, organization and personnel, which had mirrored so much else of traditional British society. The changes in the position of different industries, types and systems of employment, demands for different skills, and the pressures on types and levels of remuneration, stemming in part from these changes and in part from the growth of the consumer society, all altered the role that trade unionism 'old style' could in fact play in economic policy. The broader consequences of these developments have already been referred to earlier.

In a way it was somewhat paradoxical of the government of that period that this desire for such close co-operation with the unions went hand in hand with a more modern outlook on the realities of wage determination and its role within the general macro-economic framework. As already noticed, this was similar to the way in which the trappings of planning went together with a more pragmatic attitude to some of the ballast of 'clause four' and its belief in nationalization. In these respects the vacillations of Labour's policies were not only significant pointers for the future of the party's political philosophy, but they mirrored the general uncertainty of British policy, which, transcending the party-political spectrum, was searching for new guideposts in a world of monetary turbulence, rapid technological progress, new political alignments and a newly-emerging world pattern of economic power.

That these uncertainties and gropings were not confined to one political group is seen in the Conservative government that followed. While an increased emphasis was soon placed on individual enterprise and initiative ('Selsdon man', named after the location of the party's discussions that determined the thrust of policy), there was much rhetoric reminiscent of Wilson's 'hundred days' with emphasis on new technology and a more effective relation between science, technology, finance and industry. It was not until the advent of another Conservative government in

1979 that it appeared that a decisive break with the past zig-zag was intended, despite the early invocation of the unifying and healing power of St Francis. As we have seen, the trend of the next twelve years was much more clearly marked by attempted (if rarely fully achieved) greater fiscal stringency, greater reliance on monetary policy, a turning away from specific support for particular industries, a deliberate policy, by statute and otherwise, to diminish the influence of the trade unions and a retreat of the state from ownership and management of certain enterprises. Gradually, these policies were supplemented by attempts to reduce the scope of the 'welfare state', not only for financial reasons, but also on doctrinal grounds.

We need not go over this ground again: the main ingredients of the policy and the way it was debated in terms of the basic essentials of economic policy have already been briefly discussed. It is referred to again at this stage because of the significance which real, or perceived, radical changes of economic policy as exhibited by governments of different colour have had on economic performance.

As the country is beginning to move out of an exceptionally deep and long recession, it is difficult to form a reliable judgement on this issue. Given the persistence of high unemployment, budget deficits, unsatisfactory current account balances and as yet only modest growth it is difficult to conclude that we are witnessing anything more than another form of the stop-go cycle.

The Main Ingredients of the Problem

We are thus still left with the question of whether we can construct some kind of coherent pattern out of the sizeable number of individual explanations of inadequate performance. I have already shown why I reject the broad cultural explanation of gentrification, even if here and there specific examples of a decline of successful enterprise can be ascribed to something like the process which the theory tries to make responsible for a more generalized process of industrial decline.

The other view which points to the continued high level of performance of Britain in commercial and financial matters and argues against undue preoccupation with manufacturing is, as I have shown, also untenable. Indeed, one of the features of unsatisfactory performance which I have examined is precisely a turning away from manufacturing industry, for so long the core of Britain's economic achievement. The neglect, deliberate or unavoidable, of manufacturing, its steady decline as a proportion of the wealth-creating activities of the nation, particularly in the last two decades or so, can rightly be linked to the recurrent balance of payments problems, when repeated phases of consumption-led rather than investment- or export-led growth have quickly come up against inflationary and external balance constraints, since they lacked the powerful base of manufacturing industry and could not be sustained. Nor could the service industries, themselves subject to foreign competition as well as to technological innovation and reduced employment opportunities sustain employment, even when these made an important contribution to overseas earnings.

We are thus left with the difficult choice between either leaving the individual policy errors identified to speak for themselves, each playing a more or less important part at different times and more or less according to the taste of the beholder, or we can try to arrange these aspects in some order of significance, that is to divide them into major and minor, or principal and subsidiary causes. Neither procedure is really satisfactory. The first would leave a ragbag of issues without any clear light on how they have actually operated. The second is far too hazardous, for it would mean establishing a more stringent logical relation between, say, the alternation of expansionist and restrictionist monetary policy and the structure of the Civil Service machine than is at all obvious.

It may be useful to recapitulate briefly the different themes I have discussed and some of the broader features of governmental processes analyzed above before attempting any further linkage. I have attempted to examine a number of themes which have dominated the preoccupations of successive governments and have had the major influence on policy making together with a more or less chronological account of some of the major events of this period which can now be seen to have had a bad influence on economic performance. The themes fall roughly into two broad groups: firstly, domestic pressures on the capacity of the economy to deliver certain desirable socio-economic results – desirable as demonstrated by the electorate's attitudes towards political parties and reflected in their programmes; and secondly, external pressures, which are partly the result of internal and external economic developments, and partly stem from certain overriding claims on the economy from defence and foreign affairs requirements, as seen by the government of the day.

These show up in a variety of ways as economic phenomena, i.e. in varying allocations of national resources (either by government action or by the play of market forces) with consequences for growth, employment, inflationary and deflationary pressures, and fluctuations in the distribution of income with consequent stronger or weaker wage pressures.

The Balance of Payments Again

It is not easy to point to any one single economic development that can act as an indicator of the way in which this variegated number of issues combines at any one time. Over the greater (though not continuous) part of the period under review, the state of the balance of payments as it showed up not only in the figures of the account itself, but, from the point of view of policy makers, in the fluctuations of the exchange rate of sterling and in the state of the central foreign currency reserves, has usually been the most revealing syndrome of the country's economic state. If, as has so often been the case – indeed with alarming regularity – the attention of Ministers and officials is focused on these indicators, the policy machinery – fiscal and monetary above all – will be brought into play in the first instance. Sometimes, according to the political inclinations of different governments, all the other parts of the apparatus of government policy will be influenced by the same considerations – intervention in particular industries, regional policy, investment incentives, even funds for research, particularly into possible new industrial developments. This, of course, will only partly be so, because these areas of policy will be also heavily influenced by other broad objectives not easily subsumed under concern for the state of the balance of payments.

The overriding importance attached to the balance of payments is particularly clearly seen at certain critical points during this period. In 1925, with the return to the gold standard, it was not direct pressure on sterling or the reserves which was decisive. Indeed, the early consequence of the move was a deterioration of the export element in the balance of payments. Nevertheless, a long-term concern for the position of sterling, the strength of the financial status of the City of London, and, therefore, the longer-term outlook for the balance of payments played an important part.

Similarly, the abandonment of the gold standard in 1931, the following draconian measures of fiscal policy and also of monetary policy were also motivated by external considerations. These were even more obviously decisive at the time of the devaluation of 1949 and again in the long period of what in the Treasury was called 'the cold war' of 1963–6, which culminated in yet another devaluation. So was the exit from the European Exchange Rate Mechanism in 1992.

I have already referred to the fact that these concerns were dealt with by measures not only of external impact (exchange control being the most direct) but also by measures which affected the course of the domestic economy and its stop-go movement, together with its consequences for investment, consumption, inflation or deflation and growth. Sometimes, the latter was induced by policies stemming from domestic rather than international economic or political concerns; but they in turn, though with a time-lag, affected the external balance.

The causes for the recurrent balance of payments crises have already been briefly analyzed. In the broadest sense, they show that generally speaking the economy was called upon to deliver results well above its total capacity over the period as a whole, leading to the inevitable neglect sometimes of this, sometimes of that desirable objective. As has already been stated, the basic factor has been competition at different times for resources to meet the need to increase exports (or substitute imports) with defence or foreign policy calls – justified or not on a longer view. Often it was the competition of consumption, a relatively more easily manipulated stimulant of growth, against longer-term investment in manufacturing, infrastructure, material or human, which played the major part. As a general proposition the history of the period leads to the conclusion that the competition tended to be resolved in favour of those needs which, in terms of short-term political pressures, were the most clamorous.

At least three times during the period the overall inadequacy of our resources in the face of very large demands was relieved thus making the choices somewhat less acute, though still inevitable. The first was through the American Loan, brilliantly negotiated by Keynes. Though very small by today's values, and not on as generous terms as could have been expected, it provided immediate relief for post-war easements of living standards and reconstruction needs. Whether it could have been better used than it was is now very difficult to establish; in particular since related policies were not free from flaws, such as the settlement of sterling balances, which has already been shown to have been faulty, or the exchange rate policy, where the timing of the 1949 devaluation remains debatable.

The second relief came with the Marshall Plan, which had the very substantial advantage over the Loan Agreement that the consideration was not in terms of interest or capital repayments. However, the Marshall Plan, despite its inestimable succour to the hard-pressed balance of payments, created a more complex series of obligations in policy terms. Here again it is by no means certain that these, ranging from the forms of trade liberalization to be adopted, through currency transferability and later convertibility desiderata to the broader attitude to Europe which has already been discussed, were as appropriate to Britain's ability to effect difficult political choices as they might have been. Thus, in both cases, the immediate financial support was the main benefit.

The third relief, more fundamental than the other two, since it was independent of any foreign financial source, was North Sea Oil. It would go far beyond the scope of this essay, and has in any event been much discussed and written about, to examine the way in which this sudden and remarkable accession to our resources was dealt with, and how its apparent benefits were utilized. It must suffice to state the obvious: that the fact that so many of our problems and discontents are today not significantly different from what they were before this 'bonanza' suggests that it has not been used to best advantage.

Many of the other economic problems which have been besetting us in the last seventy years can be subsumed under the balance of payments heading. Not that the balance of payments is an independent economic difficulty, even though governments have generally treated it as such. It is more to be seen as a clear indication of the failure of the economy either through its own dynamic market forces and/or through the impact of government policy, via the budget and monetary policy, or through specific interventions in the real economy to remedy the malfunction which shows up in the balance of payments.

As I have already said, the effective contribution made by economic science to the solution of these problems over this long period is not a glorious one. It is idle to speculate whether this is primarily due to the imperfect state of the science, though this cannot be entirely set aside. Much of the blame must be laid, as we have seen, at the door of the politico-administrative process by which the theorems of economics are applied in practice. This can most strikingly be seen in the double-talk in which Ministers indulge from time to time – and not only in the understandably

125

rosy hue in which they generally paint the economic outlook. When a Prime Minister actually trained in economics can, on the occasion of a major devaluation of sterling, proclaim, 'The pound in your pocket has not been devalued,' the public's understanding of what has happened is hardly advanced. Similarly, when a Prime Minister and his Chancellor of the Exchequer can, almost to the last moment of our membership of the European Exchange Rate Mechanism, proclaim its virtues and defend the 'strong pound' policy, only to boast immediately after its abandonment of our possessing a 'fiercely competitive' exchange rate, this demonstrates not only inconsistency, but also shows ignorance of the very uncertain consequences of devaluation, of which we ourselves have had so many examples in the past. It is not too much to conclude that even if the doctrines of economics provided a surer guide to public policy than they are as yet able to do, they would not be altogether safe in the hands of politicians.

However, the short reflections on the political and administrative processes by which policy is effected which I have given earlier do not encourage the hope that reforms in those directions might ensure the avoidance of errors. Indeed, I have explicitly concluded that, while this or that improvement might be sought, any basic change in the party-political and periodic election mechanism by which we are governed is hardly likely for as far ahead as it is safe to see; nor is it clear what might advantageously replace it if change were likely.

We have seen that there have been occasions when a particular direction of economic policy has been flawed, or when a policy appropriate for the circumstances of the time has been negated by perceived political pressures which have made that policy unacceptable. We have also seen that the ups and downs of party-political fortunes and the heightened intensity of the political battle, particularly when election seems to be looming, can also turn policy in the wrong direction. It would, however, be unreasonable to ascribe what must be regarded as an unsatisfactory state over several decades as being due to some one particular cause, either strictly economic or due to specific political influences on the economy.

What seems a more reasonable conclusion is that at critical points in this history, various individual elements in our society form a noxious, sometimes even an explosive, amalgam that sets back the possibilities of economic progress for a sufficiently long time to make any subsequent recovery uncertain, short and at best feeble.

Failure to Adapt

I can think of only one possible catalyst that would explain why we have been so prone to experience these unfavourable phases, namely a very imperfect adaptability to changes in circumstances of the magnitude that have occurred during this period. It is this almost automatic reaction by traditional modes of thought and action to historically new demands that can account at one and the same time for a variety of mistakes. Thus, the fatal error of the return to the gold standard has much in common with the mistaken reaction to the crash and depression of the 1930s, which was when Keynes was already engaged in that 'long struggle of escape from habitual modes of thought and expression' that was to lead to the *General Theory* and the flowering of new economic ideas. It explains also the failure to read the European indicators aright; the belated recognition of the inevitable clash between the demands of defence and foreign policy programmes, which, even if these were justified, were not followed through either in adequate explanation or action in other areas demanding economic resources. Many more examples will readily come to mind; and these were all the more vicious in their results when they occurred at times of particularly dogmatic governmental attitudes on broader questions of economic policy, such as in the early Labour governments of the 1960s and the Conservative governments after 1979.

In an extraordinarily perverse way the remarkable victories

which the country achieved in two world wars contributed to this relative inertia in facing up to the new world pattern. The defeated or occupied countries seem to have responded more readily to the need for a new pattern of resource allocation more appropriate to the second half of the century. Our inertia in action was unfortunately rooted in a similar disinclination to think in fresh terms. Again to quote Keynes, it proved to be the case that 'the difficulty lies not in the new ideas, but in escaping from the old'.

Alfred North Whitehead, the great mathematician from Cambridge, England, who went on to become a great philosopher in Cambridge, Massachusetts, in the quotation at the head of this Part, diagnosed clearly what the long-term stability of a society requires. He did not, unfortunately, show how this difficult balance between respect for tradition and readiness to innovate can be achieved. In a larger sense, and looking at British history over a longer period, there will always be those who believe that 'revision' (in the Whitehead sense) has been too free, dangerously threatening anarchy, while others will consider it to have been too slow, raising the danger of atrophy. Britain's record over the last 250 years is good however: on the face of it, no worse than that of France, for example, perhaps the only country with a history and structure sufficiently similar to make a comparison worthwhile. There is certainly no case for saying that France has managed this difficult balancing act better.

If Britain has succeeded since, say, the Restoration and through the Industrial Revolution to preserve the basic stability of its society while absorbing major innovations into its national traditions, she has nevertheless from time to time been uncomfortably close to not achieving this balance. It is in the more recent phase, largely under the impact of greater and more rapid changes in the world setting in which the country finds itself, that the required degrees of adaptability and speed have been lacking.

The slowness of adaptation is sometimes aggravated by the fierceness with which it comes when it does. In this regard, the British economy sometimes behaves like Prince Rupert's 'drop' or phial. This small glass bottle, supposed to have been invented, or at least imported, by Prince Rupert has extraordinarily strong cohesion which makes it virtually unbreakable in the ordinary course. If, however, one of its glass 'tails' is broken, it completely disintegrates into a powder. The long-continued extolling of the old forms of specialization in the City of London, with its reliance on the 'honour system' for the protection of the average user of financial services, or the 'Governor's eyebrows' as the instrument to call financial institutions to book combined with a strong and scathing condemnation of the statutory system in the United States (the Securities Exchange Commission) gave way to a multiplicity of partly statutory partly voluntary regulatory agencies in the 'big bang'. These are examples of cherished institutions which, in a very short time, have changed or are changing most radically once a powerful initial impetus for change has been administered. Aspects of British society other than the economic show this phenomenon even more markedly.

This occasional radicalism cannot really make up for the more deliberate and systematic adaptability which Whitehead's dictum calls for. The precipitate reform almost invariably requires re-examination and revision; and where this involves legislation, it tends to run into the problems of exacerbated political debate and a strained parliamentary time-table.

The slowness of adaptation is particularly marked in the reluctance even to admit that progress has not been as good as it might have been and that errors had been made which need correcting. Politicians often tend to be particularly thin-skinned in this respect and to take refuge in the charge that critics are denigrating the country's achievements. The result is sometimes the encouragement of persistent myths which bar the way to a proper analysis. Thus it is common to hear that our unit wage-costs are among the, if not the, highest in Europe, if not in the industrial world; that on top of that our non-wage labour costs are among the highest, including in terms of percentage of GDP; that in general our welfare services, including those for health care, are the best and therefore costliest, especially when compared with those of our partners in the Community; in short that our competitiveness is poor because of high unit labour and welfare costs. Quite apart from the implicit and analytically wrong identification of unit wage and non-wage labour costs with unit cost of production none of these statements would survive even cursory scrutiny of the facts.

The output of the speech-writer, an increasingly important part of the political machine, is peppered with slogans based on such misconceptions; and policy suffers. While the European Union's latest concern with competitiveness, and in this connection the structure of labour markets, within the context of its latest study of how to promote growth and cure unemployment in a world-wide context is legitimate, the British opposition to the 'Social Chapter' of the Maastricht Treaty is not supported by either economic analysis or the facts. The longer-term gain of enlightening the electorate in these matters is not realized.

What is to be Done?

This book has been devoted to diagnosis, and the outcome is a large and varied catalogue of causes, some self-perpetuating, which can be incriminated if economic performance is judged to have been unsatisfactory. I repeat here what I have emphasized before: this is a series of indictments that could be brought against other countries too. But this also means that no ready-made answer for the broad range of mistakes can be plucked from the experience of others, even if on some particular matters their record may be worth examining for possible remedies. The difficulty of prescription lies precisely in the varied nature of the causes, ranging from inadequate clinical observation and analysis to the stubborn persistence of almost Pavlovian reactions to problems. No magical formula is available that would tackle the sum total of these problems at once, and the wearisome conclusion must inevitably be that each one must continue to be attacked patiently and steadily. The Whitehead conundrum, in particular, that runs through the whole spectrum of our discontents is not amenable to a 'quick fix'. To come closer to realizing his ideal balance requires not only progress on the various analytical, technical, administrative, social and political fronts which have been dealt with above, but also leadership of a kind which is extremely rare.

This book has dealt almost entirely with measures large and small, the output of government in the ordinary course of its business. Many have been found deficient, if not altogether contrary to the country's interest as revealed by later developments. Nothing has been said about men; and we know what George Canning and Edmund Burke had to say about 'measures not men'. I have already shown that, given the multiplicity of the causes for policy errors, remedial action by measures is very difficult. If in addition therapy has to be found in men and not only in measures, the task is beyond prescription: for this medicament cannot be commanded.

Index

134